WE WORK WHILE THE LIGHT LASTS

# WE WORK WHILE THE LIGHT LASTS

DOM HUBERT
VAN ZELLER

THE CENACLE PRESS
AT SILVERSTREAM PRIORY

First Published 1950, by Sheed and Ward, London.

This edition republished 2022 by Silverstream Priory
with the kind permission of Downside Abbey.
New material and graphic design copyright
© 2022 by Silverstream Priory.

All rights reserved:
No part of this book may be reproduced or transmitted,
in any form or by any means, without permission.

The Cenacle Press at Silverstream Priory
Silverstream Priory
Stamullen, County Meath, K32 T189, Ireland
www.cenaclepress.com

*Nihil Obstat*:
Dom Richard Davey, S.T.L., Censor Deputatus O.S.B.
*Imprimatur*:
Dom Herbert Byrne, Abbot President
11th January, 1949

*Nihil Obstat*:
Georgius Smits, S.T.D., Ph.D., Censor Deputatus
*Imprimatur*:
E. Morrogh Bernard, Vic. Gen. Westmonasteri,
Die 2A Februari, 1950

ppr 978-1-7396241-6-3

Cover and interior design by Michael Schrauzer.
Cover art: George Inness, *Moonrise* (1891), oil on canvas.

To Gerald, who will pretend that it's beyond him,
and his brother Denis, who will pretend it isn't

*The light is among you still, but only for a short time.*
*Finish your journey while you still have the light...*
*while you still have the light, have faith in the light.*
John xii. 35-6

# CONTENTS

| | |
|---|---|
| Preface | xiii |
| We Work | 1 |
| While the Light Lasts | 6 |
| Work as a Happiness | 10 |
| Work as a Discipline | 15 |
| The Law of Sin | 20 |
| The Near-saint | 25 |
| This Correspondence Has Now Ceased | 29 |
| Understanding and Misunderstanding | 35 |
| Before Marriage | 42 |
| After Marriage | 47 |
| The Marriage Problem | 51 |
| The Marriage Ideal | 58 |
| The Ideal Marriage | 63 |
| The State and the Soul | 68 |
| As with Nations so with People | 73 |
| Envy and Its Opposite | 77 |
| The Other Envy | 81 |
| Vocational Grace | 85 |
| The Schizophrenic Age | 90 |
| Sin | 94 |
| Security: the Demand for It | 102 |

| | |
|---|---|
| Security: the Mistake About It. | 106 |
| Security: Its Foundation | 109 |
| Security: Its Operation | 113 |
| Perseverance In Faith | 118 |
| Perseverance In Work | 122 |
| Perseverance In Prayer | 127 |
| Perseverance In Everything | 135 |
| Children | 141 |
| Simplicity in Art | 146 |
| Simplicity In Prayer | 150 |
| Simplicity In Everything | 159 |
| Some Practical Consequences of This | 162 |
| Case-book Question. | 167 |
| The Grace of God | 172 |
| Pendant to the Foregoing | 177 |
| Exaggeration | 182 |
| The Muffled Conscience | 186 |
| Implications of This | 190 |
| Giving | 195 |
| Giving in Prayer | 199 |
| Theme Tune | 205 |

# PREFACE

BY THE TIME THE READER HAS got half-way through this book he will have found that most of the subjects under review are, from various aspects, developments of the same theme. The question of human relationship presents more difficulties regarding the people we like than regarding the people we don't like, and if my correspondence is anything to go by, the problem which men and women living in the world most want discussed is that of how to handle the affections. It is on the evidence of my letter-writing friends that I have been led to suppose a more widespread need. If, accordingly, any correspondent of mine should happen to come across in the present work, a passage which he remembers from one of my personal letters, he is asked to take my word for it that he has not been receiving by post and addressed to him, pages of manuscript which were in fact being prepared for publication. The process, where it has been employed at all, has invariably been the reverse: having stamped the envelope, I then wondered how the thing could be put in more general terms. All this I mention here because I would rather my correspondents regarded themselves as my inspiration—which indeed they are—than as my guinea-pigs.

# WE WORK

E ARE ALWAYS BEING reminded that one of the many consequences for which Adam's sin was responsible is the unpleasantness of work. Work, before original sin, was pleasurable and recreative and satisfactory in every way; after original sin we labour with our hands and in the sweat of our brow. "It's no longer meant to be fun," we are told reprovingly, "you must expect boredom, blisters and weariness of body and spirit." This is all perfectly true. But work can be, even naturally speaking, the greatest possible blessing. It is perhaps our burden, but it is also our comfort. Sometimes it is our only comfort. To those for whom life, whether during a bad patch or over a whole course of years, is a misery, work is the appropriate anodyne.

Taken first of all simply as an outlet, the lenitive value of work can be over-prized: we can go at it simply for the drugging effect which it has on us, and not at all because it is apt. Although various energies are meant to be released by work, and although we are meant to feel the relief of having released them, it would be a mistake to look upon work simply as a means chosen by God to keep us quiet. It has a more positive function than this. The purpose of work is to sanctify the soul.

If the principle about work is mistaken, the result is likely to be the exact opposite of what was intended. Instead of promoting the soul's holiness, it can provide the most effective of obstacles. The term "work" is here understood to mean more than mere occupation. Referring primarily to what is given us to do, to what our particular profession obliges us, "work" will be taken in these pages to cover, or at least to touch, such activities as prayer, social contacts, political interests and so on. Accordingly the claim is that exaggeration in any one department of outward expression — even if the expression is specifically Godward, or as closely related to charity as to spring from natural affection — disturbs, in proportion as it exaggerates, the interior harmony which is necessary to holiness. The balance between apparently contrary loyalties must be kept level: unregulated industry, which may sometimes be nothing more reprehensible than a semi-conscientious false emphasis, can run away with the soul's peace and so prevent the operation of grace. This is very often where self-deception comes in: we tell ourselves that provided our tranquillity is not disturbed by our play or our passion there can be no harm; we think it is rather virtuous of us if our tranquillity is disturbed by our work.

In this way work can become an indulgence, an unsuspected form of luxury, an absorption which is enjoyed at the expense of prayer. Holiness is waived on the plea of the immediate need: the means is pursued as an end. Once work is established in the mind as an absolute and not a relative good, our ideas about a number of other things take on a new, and more material, character. For instance effort and output are taken to be the criterion of moral worth. They are taken to be morality itself. This is the case not only in worldly estimates but in religious ones as well. "A really Christian soul — he's at it from morning to night, and never gives himself a thought." Every day our judgements are formed along these lines. And there is excuse, too, for sizing up a man by his zeal and his time-table; these things are sometimes the only indications we've got. Moreover, saints do work unselfishly from morning till night (and it will be the main purpose of this book to get people to do the same), but it is also possible that a particular soul may work all day, not because he never thinks about himself but because he thinks about himself the whole time. Because he can't stop thinking about himself.

The value of work then, like that of penance, is relative. There are more important things. But not many. Always we have to be getting back to respective importances, respective priorities. "Seek ye first the kingdom of God, and all these things . . ." If we once make the mistake of getting our values in the wrong order, placing efficiency with its physical outlay and returns too high on the list, it is by a peculiar irony or piece of retributive justice that the work itself, to which everything else has had to give place, nearly always suffers. This need not be due, directly, to the jealousy of God who wants our effort to be referred more positively back to Him, but simply to the way in which human nature, when wrongly orientated, nearly always reacts. The expenditure of energy becomes nervous, competitive, self-regarding. The pace has to be quickened all round. The need for more and more work, more and more outlet, more and more return is like the need for mental or physical stimulant. As the appetite increases, the supply has to be provided in stronger and more frequently repeated doses. But even nature (let alone grace) is against this mounting-up process: the strain can't go at full pressure for ever. Though the will may refuse to let the soul relax and face itself in its loneliness, the body asserts itself at last and insists on slowing down. While desire for work can quite well become a mania, the physical ability to respond may decline proportionately. The powers exhaust themselves, and then there is trouble.

If our work is not a blessing it is a curse. The first evidence which we get of this is when the novelty wears off and when we tire of it. This is in the beginning. (The still earlier distaste for work which is experienced before the undertaking has properly got under way is not included as part of the curse: only what is known can be truly loathed or loved.) The second evidence of it comes much later—when the roles are reversed and when it has worn us out. It is much more of a curse now because it leaves us with nothing else to fill the gap. The effect of work immoderately indulged in is much the same as the effect of allowing any other appetite to have its unrestricted way. There is the switch over from energy to lassitude, from a full day to an empty one, from noise to silence, from climax following climax to an extended state of fatigue, flatness, and sense of failure.

In stressing the disadvantages rather than the advantages in this matter of work, the idea has been to give the obverse side of the coin first. From now onwards we can consider work as an expression of the love of God, and not as a possible hindrance to perfection or as a punishment for sin. If in the reader's mind there existed no thought of misuse or exaggeration, the pages which follow might read as unqualified exhortation to get in — feverishly and without regard to reason and the expenditure of inward capital — as many forced marches as the span of human life allowed. Qualified by the above considerations, however, the rest of this book is not likely to be misinterpreted: at any rate it will go ahead and take this opening section as accepted.

# WHILE THE LIGHT LASTS

IT CAN BE ASSUMED HERE THAT the work which we have to do in life is given us by God. It is not just a haphazard affair which we happen to find ourselves doing. Allowing then that each soul has his quota to perform, his particular block of life to hack out, his mission, there are two ways in which he may address himself to it. Both ways are sanctifying, but one way is better than the other. (There are wrong ways of approaching one's vocation, but for the moment we are considering only the right.) Thus a man may say: "Here is my job. I must put my head down and go at it. In order to make a success of it I must pray. God must be brought into it." There is nothing wrong with this; it is excellent as far as it goes. The other way goes further. "My work is God's work for me," says the second man, "so I must let it sanctify me. I shall find no sanctity apart from it. In it I shall find both happiness and God."

Holiness is not something which should be looked upon as coming on top of a man's work, sanctifying it from without and rendering it worthy to be presented to God. Rather it should be regarded as emerging out of the work, and given to God in union with it. It is not so much in virtue of our preceding prayer that the character of our work is as it were sacramentalised (though certainly this is one way of looking at it), it is rather that by bringing to our work a readiness to be sanctified by it we therein and therethrough refer the whole of our lives to God, and allow Him to work out His sanctification in us. There is a distinction here, and it would be a misfortune to miss it. Where the first way of looking at work and happiness involves calling God's blessing down upon these things, the second prefers to think of Him as so much part of work and happiness as to call for recognition in them. Where the first imposes a spiritual motive on what is undertaken, the second finds motive and inspiration in what is undertaken. The one asks God to be a safeguard, watching over our activity from outside it, the other asks God to reveal Himself more and more as the source of our activity and as its end.

The practical effects resulting from such a habit of mind are significant. Chief among them are an increased recollection kept up during the work itself, a serenity which is as proof as anything can be against disappointment, a detachment from whatever personal glory may come as the result of one's effort, and a trust that nothing can go really wrong so long as one is absolutely honest and uses the means which God gives one for the work.

Holiness, then, and happiness as well, can be found only in doing what God wants done — and in the way that He wants it done. He rewards only His own work. He provides us with just enough light to see what it is that we are to do; He then gives us the strength to do it. If we refuse to look, or, having looked, refuse to work, we are rewarded with neither holiness nor happiness. The principle is perfectly clear. We take it or leave it.

"But is it so clear?" may be the objection. "I never seem to know what to do next. Jobs come along and I take them, but I don't know that I exactly choose them as coming from the hand of God. Certainly it's seldom, if ever, that I get what you would call 'light' about my work." We may not be given much light, but we are given enough to go upon. The fact that work comes our way, and that we see enough of its implications to accept it, is light. We must work while we have the light — even if it's only a glimmer. The more ready we are to receive our works as coming from the hand of God, the more is light brought to bear. Then do we truly, though perhaps not always as consciously as we would like, work in the light. Light comes *through* our work — in the same way that we have seen holiness to come through our work. Those who turn away from God work in darkness. They haven't the light of faith. And it is the light of faith which makes all the difference, which makes it possible to go on working when there is apparently nothing to work for. Without this kind of light we can't work at all. We may be able to turn out results, but we can't *work* — in the sense understood at the beginning of this section. Our sort of work can be done only in the light of faith. The works which please God are those which are done in the light. We must work, then, for as long as the light lasts. Which means, since the light is the light of faith, that we must work till the last moment of our lives. As to how this may be realised, since for most of us the physical opportunity is likely to be denied, the essays which follow may help to suggest ideas.

# WORK AS A HAPPINESS

THERE ARE MANY WHO THINK that religion teaches people to escape the unpleasant realities of life by living in a dream world of faith. Religion, however, knows better. What religion in fact does is almost exactly the opposite: it teaches people to face unpleasant reality, and, by relating it to the reality which is supernatural, to make it into something worth while. Religion is essentially realist. It sees clearly enough the futility of trying to curtain off its subjects in a seraglio of ideas. What religion does is to persuade its subjects to bring their ideals into their outward lives, and to bring their outward lives into line with their ideals.

Where the voice of the world tells us to escape to happiness by avoiding such evils as the drudgery of routine labour, the commonplace surroundings of life, the drabness of the struggle for material existence, religion's voice gives us a more promising directive: we are encouraged to pick up the commonplace along with everything else in life and to turn it into something less drab. Escape can never be a satisfactory solution to the problem of evil. Evil runs faster than we do, and catches us up. Our only chance of finding happiness is to meet evil and come out the other side — to face unhappiness and force our way through it in the company of Christ.

Happiness, because it is essentially part of the kingdom of heaven, is within. If the kingdom's security is independent of material well-being, then the security of happiness must in the same way be beyond the reach of temporal upset. At all events religion can teach us how to make it so. The trouble is that, we imagine a happiness of our own, a happiness incompatible with the ordinary boredoms of existence — and still more incompatible with the afflictions. We think we can attain to this by eliminating all that happiness is not. We see the outward obstacles to our happiness and we begin to evade them. Either we try and slip out of their way, or (if we are braver) we try and fight them, or (if we happen to be born stupid) we deny their existence. What we do not see are the inward obstacles to our happiness. If happiness is within, so also is unhappiness. The world talks about one thing and the spirit about another. Of course the world suggests the remedy of finding satisfaction in creatures — it is the only satisfaction it is familiar with — while the spirit goes on offering a different solution altogether. There is this to be noted however: that where satisfaction in creatures can never be claimed as anything more than a remedy, satisfaction in God is held out to man as an end. The one is an antidote, the other an answer.

"What," it might be asked, "has all this to do with work?" It has this to do with work: that when the world substitutes the outward for the inward, it mistakes entertainment for happiness and the lack of it for unhappiness. Consequently the work which is found to be lacking in entertainment is looked upon as an evil. Entertainment-deficiency comes to mean the source of unhappiness. Work is not looked to any more as a possible foundation of happiness. The idea of vocation is completely missed. Labour loses its dignity as well as its opportunity. Work is something to be got through — by the unfortunate.

For the Christian it is essential that he should come to terms with work. This means that he must have clear ideas about such things as entertainment, the right use of time, the value of continuing the work even if it carries him to the last day of his life and costs him the last breath of his body. (He must have clear ideas also, if his work is to be for the honour of God and for his own happiness, about obedience, justice, and loyalty; this, however, is abundantly obvious, and hardly needs specific treatment here.)

The first thing to be got right is the place of entertainment in the scheme of existence. Surely it is meant to be the legitimate extra, the surprise reward, the more or less random accidental to life. Certainly it is not an essential of life itself. At best, and for most, it is a God-ordained adjunct. So long as it is expected casually and accepted gratefully, entertainment is in its right place. Human nature can become so voracious about it that a dislocation of emphasis can all too easily occur. We have constantly to be reminding ourselves that our happiness does not come through our entertainment but that our entertainment, if it is to be what God means it to be in our lives, comes through our happiness. Though life would certainly be dreary if we were never entertained, it would nevertheless be liveable. Like the happiness in which it is meant to subsist, entertainment comes to life as an over-and-above.

Inherent in man is the craving for happiness. His nature cries out for it. Even in his love for God he cannot dissociate himself from his love of happiness. He finds the one in the other. In all that he does he looks for happiness. Without knowing it he is looking for God. We have been told all this, and as Christians we have accepted it; it is a familiar doctrine. Yet when it comes to looking for happiness in our work, as when it comes to looking for God in our work, we forget it. We look for entertainment instead. But it is not in the nature of man to crave for entertainment; it is not his inalienable desire. Man's search for amusement, though it may be instinctive, is not constitutionally essential: it is only his permitted inclination. In his work he must look for that for which he was made, and not for that to which he feels himself inclined. In other words he must look for God and for happiness. God first, happiness second. If he divorces his work from God and happiness — imagining that he can be either religious or happy in his free time and quite apart from what has been given him to do — he misses his opportunity of both holiness and happiness. The three are merged and interact: holiness, happiness, work.

# WORK AS A DISCIPLINE

ABBOT DELATTE ONCE SAID that the three most interesting things in the world were to suffer, to wait, and to work. The application of the word "interesting" to the first two might be questioned, but there can be no doubt about its suitability as regards the third. Work can become so interesting that it can, as we have seen in the opening essay, absorb every energy. Since we cannot be happy in this world without working for our happiness, it stands to reason that there must be conditions governing both the work and the happiness. In other words there must be an ascesis about our approach; there must be a discipline. If we refuse to abide by the conditions, it means that one of the chief sources of our possible sanctity is cut off from us. Since it is largely through our work that we are sanctified, it is largely through our work that we are tempted. Thus the discipline is not merely necessary to ensure happiness, it is necessary to prevent disaster.

The ways in which our work can prove our undoing are both too many and too obvious. All that need be said here is that if we exploit it simply for self, if we exclude God from it, if we make it our excuse for neglecting everything else, if we cheat at it, if we are lazy about it, if we give it up before the time, if we make a god of it, if we drive other people to do it for us, we are worse failures in this matter of work than those whom we despise for not doing it at all. Thus for practical purposes there are two extremes which have to be guarded against: first, allowing work to run away with us; second, finding excuses for running away from it.

Experience shows that even the loftiest duties, once they have slipped from the control of right reason, can turn themselves inside out and become occasions of sin. But long before it comes to this, work can so stampede the soul as to allow no rest, no storing up of energy, no time to direct its force towards God. It can turn the brain into a machine, the hands into pistons. In the work of prayer itself there can be the over-eager workman's demand for noise. "As long as there is something going on, as long as the hammer is never still." How can prayer, real prayer, grow in such an atmosphere? Where there is too much vibration—whether in the work of prayer or in the work outside it—there can be no lasting work for God. It would be like trying to eat a sit-down meal on a platform in Victoria Station or to compose a poem while the prices are being announced on the Cotton Exchange. There is too much tension for the act of deliberate and repeated giving. Where there is great suspense, where the pace is feverish, where the conflict of ideas is overcharged, where the scene is either too fussy or too technicolour, there can be no real spirit of prayer about a man's work. It is not convenient for grace to have to compete with rush, glamour, and efficiency.

If "at my back I always hear, time's wingèd chariot hurrying near," I end up as one of two things — a hero or a nervous wreck. This sense of urgency has the effect of either stimulating endeavour and producing the worker's most significant contribution, or inducing panic which produces nothing. Always to hear the sound of chariot wheels can fret away the resilience of the mind. Spent and frayed, the sensibilities are left raw with a smarting sense of sterile frustration. People who have collapsed from overwork (or from overstraining their heads at prayer) find themselves harassed by the least thing. They can do nothing with alacrity. All sorts of dreads, shrinkings, phobias, inhibitions, declare themselves: the smallest obligations haunt them with the sense of their incapacity: they find it almost impossible to get through their ordinary duties: decisions, responsibilities, commitments are felt to be unbearable.

Often when the springs of resolution have been broken, it is not because there has been too much work but because there has been too much business about doing it. It is not the amount which reduces us, or even the time which we give to it, but the state of mind in which we do it. Work which is done with one eye on the clock is bound to be either smothering or boring; work which we are worried about or which we feel to be beyond us, work which we are afraid of or which we do in bad faith, work which divides our minds and claims conflicting loyalties cannot but be in excess of the strain which work is intended by nature and grace to involve.

The second necessity (which is that of actually doing it, and not getting someone else to do it instead, or allowing it to go undone) is no less important. This brings in the discipline of time where before it was the discipline of appetite. In a quite exceptional Archers' story called *A Matter of Life and Death*, the young airman-poet is allowed to go on with his life after a period of suspension on the understanding that he will not waste the time that is being given him beyond his allotted span. The defending counsel gives the guarantee that his client will go on writing poetry, and trying to improve upon whatever he produces, for as long as his time of restored life shall last.

On the pain of greater labour a man may not lay down the burden which has been given him. Indeed the principle can be carried further, for even if no actual burden is laid upon a man by Providence there will be the intolerable labour of *ennui* to put up with if he does not find one for himself. It is a curious paradox that labour is one of the conditions of mental ease. This is perhaps less surprising when we realise that happiness is to be found in carrying the cross. Without the yoke there can be no true sweetness: we know the meaning of lightness only when we have become familiar with the weight of burdens. Pleasure cannot lend the taste to life for anything like as long as can labour. "If thou wilt be happy for a day," says a Chinese proverb, "visit the barber and the baths. If thou wilt be happy for a week, marry a wife. If thou wilt be happy for a month, buy a horse. If thou wilt be happy for a year, either write a book or build thyself a house with thine own hands. Beyond this time there is no created thing which can ensure thy happiness." For most people there is work which has to be done. Let them do it and thank God for it. For the rest there is the obligation of finding a work which will be more than a hobby and less than a slavery. With these the problem is more acute than with the others. It is for them to pray that the right work may come along, and, when it has come along, to do it with even more gratitude and sense of mission.

# THE LAW OF SIN

WHEN ALLAN MONKHOUSE makes one of his characters in *Mary Broome* say "I am not like the things which I do," he is echoing St. Paul's complaint about the law of sin in his members. "What I do is not what I wish to do," the saint tells the Romans, "but it is something which I hate." Yet we are like the things we do—or we would never dream of doing them. We *do* wish to do them—or we would never explain about hating it. "My action does not come from me," is St. Paul's agonised appeal, "but from the sinful principle that dwells in me." It is our tragedy that we can all too easily identify ourselves with the sinful principle which dwells within us, that we can sympathise with it, that we can enter into it, that we can help it to gain its effect. Both St. Paul in his epistle and Mr. Monkhouse in his play admit that we can grow into that which we hate. To "the evil which my will disapproves" (the words are St. Paul's, not Mr. Monkhouse's) I am able to sacrifice my integrity, my ideal, my character, my talent, my vocation. And all the time it will be to me, the real me, that the sacrifice is being made. *I* shall be sacrificing myself—to *me*.

"Praiseworthy intentions are always to hand," St. Paul goes on, "but I cannot find my way to the performance of them." This is indeed the supreme humiliation — that the consciousness of sin is often far more vivid than the consciousness of divine assistance. "The evil is close at my side," admits the saint. We breathe in a polluted atmosphere. We loathe it but we breathe it in. Everything has been tainted by the Fall. Not even nature is perfectly fresh. The innocence of children is the purest thing in the world, but even babies arrive in the wash of original sin. We have to go to our Lord and our Lady if we want to find what the world has not been able to touch.

"Evil is close at my side": hell is precisely this. Hell is the state of being cut off from all contact with God — even with such indirect contact as may be maintained in this world by a sinner who, though he may not be able to live up to it, at least wants the good which he sees in people better than himself — and being obliged to go on living for ever in sin. What must be the dreariness (let alone the other evils inherent in the state) of having nothing on which the mind can fasten with any sense of appreciation? Nothing to love, and nothing from which a return of love can possibly be evoked. On earth one might conceivably get used to living in a state of constant mortal sin; on earth one might either distract oneself or harden oneself; one might eventually, or at all events for considerable periods of time, forget about it. Hell is essentially the state of being unable to get used to living with evil. Hell is the continued pressure of evil. Not only the pressure of evil against good, but of evil against evil; it is the pressure of everything against everything else.

We are told that the worst consequence of sin is the sense of loss. We think of loss as something negative. Assessed strictly, and in finite terms, this is correct. It is having to do without. Hell is having to do without God, without love. We try and imagine what this must feel like by remembering the occasions in life when we have had to do without God and without love. We pick out those days of loneliness from the past and multiply them to infinity. We think of human loneliness first, and then attach a supernatural significance to it. This is the way our minds work; it is the only means at our disposal; we form our ideas about divine loneliness by looking at the kind which we know all about. What happens when people leave us? Does not pain weigh upon us out of the sky, meet us round every corner, whisper at us from the leaves of every tree, press against us whenever we open a door, jab at us when we kneel to pray, when we sit down to eat, when we wake in the morning and when we go to bed? Who would claim that this is a purely negative emotion? Emptiness can reach the stage of filling the soul with sorrow. It is a positive ache. But whether the yearning of loneliness is positive or negative, the point is that of all the feelings which human beings experience it is the one which most often remains, clear cut and poignant, in the memory. When we have forgotten almost every other agony, physical and mental, the peculiar dread of loneliness can continue to haunt us in retrospect. Even doubt and fear (those other two human horrors) are seen in terms of loneliness: they are aspects of it: if we were not alone with our doubt and our fear we should certainly not feel their misery to anything like the same extent. Loneliness, humanly speaking, is without exception the most searching of trials, and the most comprehensive. Gethsemani teaches us this.

It is from Gethsemani that we learn what it must be like not only to do without the understanding and sympathy of those who are nearest to us in friendship, but also to do without the sense of God's protection. If in our own experience we feel as we do when left alone to cope with even the ordinary wastes of life — apart altogether from its sufferings — what must it not feel to know that God, in whom is all that is lovable, is leaving us alone for ever? It is not that God drives us out from His friendship, but that we drive Him. We bear about in our mortal bodies the motive force which can expel God for ever. The principle of sin, which St. Paul says is natural to us, can pass an eternal life sentence. Man passes it — upon himself. No wonder St. Paul, awed by the loneliness which his contemplation of sin brings before him, exclaims with a groan: "Pitiable creature that I am, who is to set me free from a nature thus doomed to death?" We have still, while life remains to us, the Apostle's hope which answers unshakably: "Nothing else than the grace of God, through Jesus Christ our Lord."

St. Paul's struggle, tossed as the saint is between hope and despair, is nowhere better heard than here in his Epistle to the Romans. "My conscience is at God's disposal," he concludes, "but my natural powers are at the disposition of sin." Hence the dreadful uncertainty which we have to carry with us through life—the feeling of never being quite sure that we shall not let sin get the upper hand. Surely this sense of sin's imminence, the knowledge that our natural powers will go on being subject to the lure of sin for as long as there is breath to animate the body, must constitute one of our worst trials. Certainly it calls for the highest act of trust. Trust, on St. Paul's showing, is indeed the only solution. The "disposition of sin" was even more vivid to him than it is to us; but what mattered was "putting his conscience at God's disposal." Unless we give grounds for it, the law in our members can never condemn.

# THE NEAR-SAINT

NE OF THE SADDEST things in the world is for a man or woman to have the flair for heroic sanctity, but not quite enough of it. When you read Bossuet or Francis Thompson or Tauler or Richard Rolle or Father Baker, you say: "This man ought to be a Saint." You wonder why these people, and a lot of others, are not saints. You do right to wonder; it is very strange. But why do you not wonder the same about yourself?

The hunger for sanctity is not a rare phenomenon: it is granted to most who know anything of God at all. Without it the religious life would never be embarked upon—let alone maintained. It is a desire which can be blown into flame more readily in some than in others, and certainly it is one which can be damped down where no effort is made to keep the glow alight, but at least in some sort of smouldering form the fire exists in most of us. It *can* go cold and turn to ashes, but it is only waiting for a touch and it will answer with a firework shower of sparks. Sparks are not everything, but they are a good enough preparation for a blaze.

By the time most of us are forty it has become abundantly clear that we are failures. (Which, incidentally, is one reason why we are so pitiably eager in middle age to parade whatever outward success we have managed to achieve; it is the law of occult compensation.) This consciousness is to be found not only among religiously minded people, who might be supposed to possess an extra fund of humility, or among the hyper-sensitive, who might be suspected of suffering from a disappointment-fixation, but just as much among men and women who appear on the surface to be triumphantly successful. The truth is that all of us know in our heart of hearts how very far we have fallen short of what once we could have been. Whatever our friends think of us, whatever our material contribution, nothing can balance our moral failure. Not merely our moral insufficiency, but our moral failure. There may be some in whom this melancholy awareness is part of a non-fulfilment complex; in nearly everyone, however, it is fact.

Now if the above is the case as regards failing to realise ideals in the human order, it is still more true of ideals which relate to the spiritual life. What monk or nun can claim that the high hopes entertained in the novitiate have been verified? Who can look at those early retreat-notes without a very real — and not merely an emotional — sense of shame? Who, whether under vows or in the world, can compare without uneasiness the standards which were his when he first understood the implications of religion with the standards which he allows himself now?

To deny, for whatever reason, the early appetite for holiness is to provide for a recurrent and sometimes nightmarish hunger later on. Deliberately to turn down the offer of sanctity creates a famine in the soul which no amount of compensations can satisfy. In fact, the more we pour other things into the void, the more empty do we feel our lives to be.

A grace which has been declined sets up, by its very absence, an inflammation which has all the pain-inflicting qualities of penance without any of its merit. Unless the soul decides to put the clock back, to ask God for a return of the same invitation which was heard and rejected long ago, the mortification of mere regret is of little value. Sorrow for past infidelity is of value only in so far as it is effective. It is no good just being sorry if there is no regard whatever to the future. In this way remorse of conscience may be endured without the least satisfaction of knowing that it is being useful. The sense of guilt is disquieting and dispiriting, where it should be leading up to purposes of amendment. Such contrition is not contrition at all; it is a good emotion wasted.

In many souls there are all the yearnings after prayer and penance and a greater generosity which would be enough to set off a whole army of potential saints on the way to God. But there is just something missing, without which such yearnings are so many soap bubbles. What is it that we—all of us—lack? Is it courage? The first necessity is perhaps courage, but there is more in it than merely being brave. Where we fail most is in the quality of our faith—and by faith is meant a composite virtue consisting of hope, love, perseverance, trust, unselfishness, generosity and consistency. It is the virtue by which the just man lives. Faith is not merely belief in the existence of God and the truth of the Gospel; it is living in the image of God and by the light of the Gospel. The life of faith is life in Christ, and since we are unwilling to give ourselves fully to this life we remain as we are — mediocrities.

Perhaps in God's mercy the acknowledgment of our ungenerosity will be reputed for penitence of heart. Possibly, too, our ineffectual longing for holiness (of a sort) will be allowed to count as the authentic thirst for Christ and justice and the Father's will. Let us hope that this may be so, but let us not hope it too much — and take advantage of it. Such a hope would take us back again to our excuses, to our rejections.

To conclude. It may be better to go through life without the least awareness of a supernatural vocation than to have an attraction which is *only* an attraction. Our Lord told the Jewish leaders that they had now no excuse for their sin. To them had been given the light. The others, the casual members of the national religion, had never really seen. It was the enlightened who were to blame. Everything depends upon the right use of light. It is for us to work while there is the light. Without labouring at our sanctification we cannot be sure, however spiritual our dreams, that these strong desires of ours, which are not quite strong enough, will qualify.

# THIS CORRESPONDENCE HAS NOW CEASED

EARLY ALL OUR TROUBLE with other people—people we are fond of—is due to the fact that our natures cry out against the maddening limitations of being human. When our relations with others go wrong it is because we refuse to allow that our demands have been exorbitant. This is not merely to say that we should take a tolerant view of our friends, turning a blind eye to their mistakes and not letting ourselves be hurt when we find them falling short of the ideals which we have woven round their characters; it is to go much deeper than this: it is to say that our mistake lies in trying too hard and too selfishly to exact from our friends a manifestation which we have absolutely no right to claim.

In dealing above with the question of work, we have seen how the driving lust for creative activity can defeat itself by inducing disorder, sterility, listlessness. In the same way the force which longs too eagerly to express itself in the quest for human affection can exhaust itself and find nothing but a desperate dissatisfaction. "We don't keep up with each other. We've drifted. We were both very different, and it wasn't worth it." So these dreary tragedies repeat themselves.

Thirsting for a response from the material world, and finding after years of trial that the material world is incapable of making this response, we are faced with one of three choices. We can take the cynical view, and say "In that case nothing is worth while"; we can take the idealist view (which is at the same time a perfectly realist view) and say, "In that case the more we make of the material world — in expectation of full satisfaction in a spiritual world — the better"; or, thirdly, we can go on with our quest in the vague hope that somehow we shall find what we want here below. Since the majority of mankind seem, whatever their theoretical opinions, to adopt this last course (and since the idealist view will be dealt with at length in the next volume of this series, *We Sing While There's Voice Left*), we can confine our present study to the process whereby human nature continues to break its face against the problem of deriving satisfaction from what is necessarily unsatisfying.

At the beginning, in our early years of search, we are restless. We see possibilities opening up all round us. There are mountains to climb and heroes to worship. We are intolerant of routine, commonplace people, grey surroundings. We want to get on with the business of life: our life: the life we are choosing: we, we, we. Then we try climbing our mountain and worshipping our hero. Success may or may not come to us, but even if it does it is not as satisfying as we had hoped; there seems to be something missing. We go on with our search — this time perhaps there is another mountain and another hero. Again the sense of insufficiency. Rather than lower our next mountain and change the label on our next hero, we repeat the attempt. But always we seem to be back again among just those things which we despised and which made us impatient at the start. Of course. It must be so. We are back at routine, commonplace people, grey surroundings, because we are back at life: because we are back at *ourselves*. Life is not all mountain top and hero because *we* are not all mountain top and hero. We are human, insufficient, fickle, pitiable, questing, groping, unsatisfying to others no less than to ourselves, incapable of finding rest in created things.

Later on in middle age — the early spirit of adventure showing signs of wear — the mood of restlessness is added to by the sense of waning hope. Not always is this a resentful habit of mind, a feeling of frustration: it is more often the feeling that since none of one's dreams has been realised in the years when they stood their best chance, the prospect of their being realised now, when one is only too miserably awake, is not encouraging. But one goes on, all the same, trying to find one's heaven on earth. One never really learns.

There is now, however, an altered scale of values in one's approach. By now the showy successes are less desired than some of the more settled satisfactions which success may be expected to provide. One doesn't want possession so much as peace. One doesn't want fame so much as security in the minds of one's immediate circle.* One doesn't want looks or charm *as such* — either for oneself or in others — but loyalty and affection. Yes, above all, one wants reciprocated affection. Thus in the last analysis even beauty, even youth, even intelligence, are found to be unsatisfying as such. What our natures are craving for is a response, and if these other things exist outside ourselves and show no tendency to get in touch with us, we feel them to be no use. By their want of correspondence they merely aggravate. We want to absorb them, not admire at a distance. If this is shown in our dealings with inanimate good, it is shown more clearly still in our relations with human beings. There seems to be a law of potential affinities whereby the failure to comprehend absolutely, results in apparently infinite separation. It is this infinite gulf between our desire and our possession that makes all earthly happiness such a hide-and-seek affair. Mutual comprehension is never absolute.

Thus the human urge to assimilate, to pin down, to control, is at the back of all our frustrations and most of our estrangements. The urge defeats itself. The natural instinct, by going beyond its object, recoils and contributes to its own hurt. It is always this fatal note

---

\* Tacitus says that the last of mortal infirmities to be discarded is ambition. Most people over the age of about forty would be inclined to dispute this.

of demanding that spoils our enjoyment of created happiness. Possessed by this hankering for a return which experience tells us again and again we shall never receive, we go on feeling empty all our lives. We know that without a complete return we shall be infinitely removed from what we want. Yet we go on wanting it. We go on looking for at least a return of some sort. It is plumb foolishness, but we go on all the same.

As we grow older the truth is borne in upon us that nothing short of the Beatific Vision can satisfy us. We have been told this all our lives, but there comes a time when we know it for ourselves. People don't have to tell us any more. Seeing, however, in the radiance of reflected love an iridescence which we think will vivify the grey flatness of prosaic things, we press for an experience which will not only absorb us utterly but which will also absorb someone else. In effect, we never really learn.

The reason why we sometimes allow our closest friendships to be broken up is because we cannot be content with simply having the other person; we want the other person's feelings as well. We clamour to know what is going on in the other's mind; we think that without an inventory of the other's emotions and mental processes, the relationship cannot survive; we claim such knowledge as our due. Whether or not we ourselves would be prepared to come forward with our minds an open book is not strictly to the point; the point is that we must take people in their terms of reference and not in ours. The right to comprehend is reserved to God: human beings are His, not ours. Our friends are made in His image, not in ours.

"We got on very well together at one time. Perhaps we were too devoted. Anyway it didn't work. And now we've parted." With its two-edged sword and its imponderable balances, the law of potential affinities can separate for ever, and by spaces of infinite misunderstanding, souls who were meant to spell each other's happiness. The same law can also, when properly handled, unite them.

# UNDERSTANDING AND MISUNDERSTANDING

IN THE FOREGOING SECTION we concluded that people were to be liked for what they were, and not for what they could give us by way of satisfaction or for what we hoped to make of them. When the saints tell us that we are no more than what we are in the sight of God, they are not only impressing upon us the need for humility (which in any case we might have guessed) but suggesting also that because human beings are responsible to God before they are responsible to each other, they must not make the mistake of appropriating one another for even the laudable but misconceived purpose of re-shaping character. How can we possibly know for certain that our idea about the proposed perfection of any one individual is the same as God's idea? God gives us our friends in order that they and we may mutually benefit; He wants influence but not possession. There is no harm in our wanting to make our friends more worthy to be presented by us to God, but the first concern is to see them as they are presented by Him to us. They belong to Him; they are only lent to us.

Proverbially blind in assessing the quality of those to whom we are attached, we are liable to make two mistakes. Sometimes both at the same time. The first comes from either over- or under-confidence, the second from the habit of generalisation. As regards the first we may leave aside the question of over-confidence because the consequences — such as sentimentality, unwarranted assumptions, subsequent disillusion and many others — are generally understood; it is chiefly with the question of underestimating the nature of the relationship that we are here concerned. As regards the second — the tendency to make sweeping judgements — the mistrust to which it gives rise, is much the same as the mistrust which is occasioned by the want of confidence already mentioned; but because the process of arriving at it is different, the two approaches can be discussed separately.

Finding that others do not reveal themselves as fully as we would like, we mentally accuse them of being secretive and deceitful. ("I, on the other hand, am always so absolutely open. Perhaps that's just why I simply can't understand it when people aren't open with me. If only everyone were as frank as I am.") More often than not the truth is that the other's silence is adopted on a principle which is quite as lofty as the principle of keeping nothing back. But whether the reserve is deliberately practised as a safeguard or whether it is suggested instinctively by an uncommunicative nature, it is by no means a quality which is opposed to the self-giving which is required for love or friendship. The reverse of generosity is selfishness, not reticence. In those yellow moods of doubt which come upon us in our dealings with even the people we are most fond of, we must guard against confusing restraint with concealment. The presumption is that we ourselves are not restrained enough.

To question happiness is to lose the sense of it. Yet in our relationships we are always doing this: we question either our own happiness or the other person's. We want to know too much. The knowledge of it is something which the relationship can well do without. To start wondering about the security of any union, whether as regards its present foundations or its future chances, is already to undermine it: the happiness of human relationships must be taken for granted. This is not to say that the idea of mutually contributing happiness is to be ignored; it is to say that it must not be inspected. The happiness of the whole is dependent upon the happiness of the parts. But the way to bring this about is not for the parts to work out their own happiness and hope for the best, it is for the parts to forget about their own happiness and think only of the happiness of the whole. Which in practice means thinking of the other person's. This principle applies to the union of a number of people as well as to the union of only two. Thus if in a family or a community one member makes it his concern to provide for the happiness of a lot of people and to forget his own, he stands a chance of effecting many happinesses (as well as his own) where otherwise he stands a chance of bringing about no more than a doubtful one.

Turning now to the second obstacle which blocks the way in this matter of mutual harmony, there is the aptitude, which is more highly developed in some than in others, whereby individuals are seen too much as types and where the types are so rigid that non-conformity, however accidental and insignificant, is either simply not understood or else taken to be a flat contradiction in the particular person's essential nature. It is the inability to view people's characters "in the round." We see people, again to speak sculpturally, as in high or low relief; we do not think of them in more than one plane. We do not admit, because we do not see it at once, that there can be another side. But people are not just two dimensional, or three; they have sides which should not only be revealing themselves in unpredictable profusion as we get to know the people better, but which also must be accepted on faith, guessed at, made allowances for, accepted at their highest valuation rather than at their lowest, and not pried into without necessity and leave. Back again, then, at this question of reticence and the rights of privacy. Let others unfold their natures spontaneously in the course of the relationship, but either to deny that there is anything more to unfold (in the belief that we have seen all there is to see and that this is covered by the type which we have preconceived) or to probe about for qualities which we suspect to be present but of which we want confirmation (again in the belief that we know the type) is fatal.

It is the penalty of clear-cut minds that they are inclined to see both themselves and other people in over simplified forms. It is their self-judging faculty which is as much to blame as their misunderstanding of others. Having in the abstract reduced each kind of personality to a formula, they make each person fit it in the concrete. Good people, to them, are good all through; bad people are wholly bad. But people are simply not *like* this. They protrude. They overlap into other types. Fallen nature cannot be complete any more. Not even original sin can ensure complete badness; not even sanctifying grace can ensure complete goodness.

The fault about these mistaken approaches lies in having enough idealism to make for unreality and not enough to make for truth. The saint, who is the finished idealist, knows that people are not either all sheep or all goat; we, ready to imagine the whole from an incomplete part, separate the two absolutely. Sheep can be depressingly goatlike, and goats can be surprisingly like sheep. Fields may be judged by their wheat, but it is absurd to pretend that there is no cockle. It is easier to think of people as black or white, diabolical or angelic, and so we do it. "He gave himself away at once. I sized him up the first moment I met him. A thoroughly unpleasant individual." Wrong though such condemnations may be, they do at least allow for the glad shock of discovering that we have been mistaken. The opposite conception on the other hand, admitting no clay in the composition of our hero, lays itself open to hopeless disillusion and disappointment. It is both unreal and unfair to come to our friends — or to our enemies for the matter of that — with a ready-made character for them to conform to.

To conclude. In order to get on with those whom we admire and like we should not demand a consistency which nature is incapable of giving. If we would see our friends in any other terms but our own, we must accustom ourselves to the humiliation of watching the haloes which we have designed for them bent into unexpected shapes. With prayer rather than with protest must we watch such development. Always at the back of our minds must be the knowledge that failure is not conclusive, and that evil tendencies, weaknesses of character, crass foolishness, extraordinary lapses, ingratitude, selfishness and meanness, are compatible with principles which are fixed and absolute. So long as we can be sure of the will to be good, we need not be shocked by aptitude to be bad. Are not we ourselves exactly this mixture? By blinding ourselves to the evidence in our own case, we fail to see the same combination of elements where it exists in someone else. If only our self-criticism were more searching and more sure we would cease to feed ourselves on dreams. Self-deception weaves fantasies round more lives than merely our own, and the sooner we can acknowledge without cynicism that life as a whole must be less lovely than we are capable of imagining, the better for ourselves and for those we love. But unfortunately so many of us, preferring fantasy to fact and pursuing beauty beyond the limits of our ridiculously finite state, doom ourselves to bored and boring disappointment.

# BEFORE MARRIAGE

EVEN ALLOWING THAT THEY have high standards beforehand and are properly prepared for what they have taken on, married people find life difficult enough; but for those who drift into it with no very fixed ideas the married state must present mental shocks and struggles which, if one is left to face them alone, are enough to induce disillusion, cynicism, recklessness. It is an astonishing fact that young men and women can blunder their way into the most important condition of their lives: a strong emotion, a snap decision, no instruction, and then the discovery that they did not know what it was all about. Often it is too late after marriage to start working out a principle regarding it; the thing is left to look after itself, and experiment is allowed to take the place of previous preparation. All this is hardly less harmful to married happiness than the evil of experimenting, in order to judge whether the married act is harmonious or not, during the period of engagement. These two wrong approaches to matrimony may be dealt with separately.

In the first place it is not enough to get together a few edifying thoughts about unselfishness and mutual assistance and self-control when the process of being in love has already got under way. The whole trouble about falling in love is that one loses one's balance; one is inclined to lose one's head as well as one's heart. Principles have to be firmly rooted before the process begins. The Church's views — Christ's views therefore — must be known, must be accepted as absolute, must be the condition of the whole undertaking. Catholics should grow up in the state of mind which takes Christian ideals, laws, practices for granted. From childhood this mentality should be built up, got used to, worked into the system, prayed about, so that when love comes along there will be no stampeding of the judgement and weakening of the will. Love is such a sweeping force that unless the soul is prepared for it the anchorages are torn away. For the time being there is blindness; the gospel principles are not seen. And yet it is now more than ever that the gospel principles must be sought for and lived. To a man or girl who is rapidly falling in love the knowledge that certain necessities are fixed and right, certain practices forbidden and wrong, is vital if there is to be any hope of married happiness.

As regards the other pre-matrimonial menace to future security, it can be seen at once that a love which experiments beforehand will be just as ready to experiment afterwards. And possibly with someone else. The love which is not strong enough or noble enough to restrain either one's own or the other person's passion before marriage will certainly not be of the quality to survive the strain that will be put upon it later on. Clearly if he or she looks for an experimental assurance which no anticipation of marriage is meant to provide, there is not only at once a denial of the supernatural character of the future union — with the act of faith as one of its conditions — but there is also the explicit admission that he or she cannot protect the other from the sensual in both their natures. If the ceremony of marriage comes after this, it comes more as a concession than as a sacrament. To drag in the wedding as an afterthought, having proved the act of marriage to be mutually agreeable, is not merely to reverse the right order: it is to violate the purpose. It means that the lower is given greater weight than the higher, that the animal has had a start over the rational. In marriage each one owes it to the other to safeguard their mutual rights as human, not as animal, beings. Human beings are united by rational, not by bestial, ties. The rights of married people are governed by nature helped out by reason and law; they are not dependent on carnal instinct. A man is not even the possessor of his own body — let alone anyone else's — and may not claim, therefore, to do what his body urges him to do: the body has no rights which are not given to it by the spirit. In this matter of natural union the spirit dictates to the flesh through the sacrament of matrimony.

Since, moreover, marriage is designed by Providence as a life — a state of being and becoming, and not merely as an act or series of acts — the worst possible way of embarking upon that life is by the premature exercise of what is meant to be its final consummation. The appropriate act of marriage is appropriate only in marriage: only in marriage is it the expression of the habit of love. For the climax to come in advance of what it is intended to perfect and culminate is an inversion which cannot but promote similar inversions all along the line. The initial exercise of the act is, putting aside for a moment its significance in the spiritual order, of such profound importance in the psychological make-up of both parties that, should it take place outside the state of matrimony (or, inside matrimony, under conditions running counter to its true nature), there is every likelihood of the sex-conscience being permanently warped. To start off wrong on such a vital issue is to prejudice the chances of thinking right—let alone acting right—in the future. The relationship leaves the sacramental level before it has a chance of knowing what advantages Christian marriage claims to provide. By sin the right to that happiness which the sacrament offers is waived: momentary pleasure is chosen in the place of settled peace. Men and women may not afterwards claim what they have done their selfish best earlier on to stifle. By deliberately following their lusts they have renounced what nature and grace intended for them, and it is no good their complaining about it when the ardour has cooled and when they are looking round for a happiness which is more lasting. For the woman the mental and physical upheaval occasioned by the first use of the act may be more fundamental than for the man, but for each of them it is both so significant and so sacred that to perform it lightly, indifferently, cynically or brutally is to do something which is more than merely wasteful or meaningless: it is to do something which is monstrous. It is as monstrous for him as for her. It is a travesty. It is happiness committing suicide.

# AFTER MARRIAGE

PERHAPS FOR THE PRESENT purpose the clearest way of looking at married life is to base our discussion upon the difference which exists between the love of the man and the love of the woman. If both are aware of their own natural tendencies they may be more ready to adjust themselves to the conditions of their married life. The muddle comes when each leaves the direction to the instinct of the moment or to the other person. In this respect the wife is usually the worse off because she more naturally, and rightly, takes the lead given by the husband. So if the husband's instinct is wrong, or if his principles are weak, or if his desires get out of control, the wishes of the wife are overridden and there is failure. It should be a help, therefore, if each is clear as to what particular instincts and handicaps are natural to the respective sex.

From the outset the things which a woman looks for in her love are of a quieter kind than what is wanted by the man. Where she wants affection, peace, a settled place in the life of the one she loves, he more directly wants her. For the man it is more the immediate expression of his love, and its satisfaction, which dominate. Later on, when he has got used to the idea of love and when life has taught him a certain wisdom, he comes to want what she does; but to start off with he thinks of love first as a hunger which needs gratifying, and then only as reciprocated devotion and trust. The man's love, therefore, expresses itself more violently; its reactions are quicker; it carries him away in a rush. The woman's may be just as emotional, just as greedy and possessive in the long run, but it is normally more calculating than the man's: she doesn't lose her head quite so easily. The consequences of this are important. It means first that the woman's part is not intended either by nature or grace to be a purely passive one; on the contrary the woman is meant, because of her more clear-minded response to the emotion, to exercise a directing influence. Less tempted by what is specifically of the flesh, the woman can call a halt when the flesh is seen to be getting its own way. The man, by that time, may not be able to. Or at all events he will find it a lot more difficult. Though the man's part in the marriage is that of the ruler, and though the responsibility is in the last analysis more his than hers, the rights and obligations are, after all, shared. If it is for him to rule, it is for her to guide. By her attitude towards the intimacies of marriage the woman is able to influence the general trend of it in a way which very often she is unwilling to admit. On her rests the obligation of steering her husband's love into the right course if it should at any time go wrong. It is within her power, on the other hand, to deflect it and make of it something of this earth only. All the more blame to the woman, therefore, if either before marriage or after, she incites in a man a desire which it may not be in her power to meet or control. This is unfair on him. It is no good saying afterwards: "But I knew exactly where *I* stood . . . it isn't my fault if he goes too far . . . why can't he behave as I do?" What the woman has to realise is that the man is made differently, and that very often this difference is responsible for a good deal of unhappiness and evil which could be avoided. Because a woman can draw a line at any given point, this is no reason why a man can do the same. It is often the woman's temptation to see how far she can take the man's desire without herself committing sin. Having brought it the required distance, she then says it may go back again. But what happens if it won't? Too late then to complain that she's disillusioned, disgusted, repelled. She's asked for her disappointment. Adam may have put the blame on Eve for the sin of disobedience, but it is nearly always Eve who puts the blame on Adam for the sins of sex.

Thus whether from vanity, curiosity, jealousy, loneliness, boredom or from the sheer love of making mischief and playing with fire, women are prone to egg a man on until he is virtually — though never actually and absolutely — defenceless. Most women know very well that they can, without much difficulty, wring what is base and what is secret from a man, Love is at once the most delicate thing in the world and the most potentially gross. Perhaps it is because the woman is more conscious of its delicacy than of its grossness that she does not fear to take such risks. Perhaps this to some extent excuses her. The man, less naturally conscious of love's sensitive excellence, is not so ready to consider what it is that he is asking of the woman. Be this as it may, the ideal of love must remain the same for both of them. Nor is there one ideal before marriage and another after. Thus it would be equally wrong for either man or woman to rouse in the other before marriage the passion which has to be carefully watched even after it.

# THE MARRIAGE PROBLEM

PROBLEMS COME UP IN THE first week of married life, and are either solved or shelved; the real problem comes up later on, and, without being consciously shelved, is perhaps never satisfactorily solved. Indeed it is difficult to see how the problem of two people permanently living together can be perfectly solved—any more than the problem of the spiritual life can be perfectly solved. The whole thing depends upon the degree of unselfishness which is brought to bear. When people say to you (and they are always saying it): "I would give anything to get my marriage right," ask them if they would give themselves. It was self, after all, that was mutually handed over at the altar steps. But people are not prepared to abide by what they said at the altar steps. The same thing happens in the spiritual life: "I would give anything to be a saint—except of course my own will."

But though the marriage problem can never be fully solved because people are never wholly selfless, there must be, and there is, a degree of unselfishness to which men and women may hopefully attain and which will guarantee as satisfactory a solution as anyone has a right to on earth. It will provide, in other words, human happiness. The right to this married happiness, which includes the joys of bringing up a family and experiencing the security of having a home of one's own, is proportionate to the willingness to keep the rules. In another chapter, when the family will be considered as such, the value to happiness which is given by the indissolubility of marriage must be dealt with; for the present, however, some of the more subjective elements which go to the solving of the marriage problem deserve attention.

Let us begin at the beginning. Christ takes human love and makes a sacrament out of it. Human love, by taking the sacrament and making a family out of it, renders to God an account of its stewardship. Love is God's gift which man may enjoy, paradoxically, only when he is prepared to give it back. By sharing it with the donor he possesses it; by hoarding it and spending it on himself he loses the joy of it. Marriage can be the success which God means it to be only when the sacramental character is accepted and lived up to. "But these standards are altogether too lofty and unpractical. If everyone behaved before marriage and after marriage in the way suggested, the world would be full of married saints. It is unreasonable to expect the ideal from ordinary people living in the world. The kind of marriages which you have in mind are beyond human nature." The demands of Christian marriage *are* unreasonable — that is why Christ turned the union into a sacrament. Christian marriage is beyond human nature — that is the whole point. If Christian marriage could be kept up to the right level without the help of supernatural grace there would be no need of the sacrament. The sacrament is there to make humanly possible — and possible in the widest sense of being attainable to any who take the trouble to obey the conditions — what by nature the majority of mankind would infallibly get wrong.

St. Paul's eighth chapter to the Romans can be applied to the attitude of the Christian towards marriage. "The spiritual principle of life has set me free, in Jesus Christ, from the principle of sin and of death. There was something the law could not do, because flesh and blood could not lend it the power; and this God has done by sending us his own Son." Left to ourselves we cannot solve the problem of living together without sin or infidelity: the pull of nature is all the other way. "To live the life of nature is to think the thoughts of nature," says St. Paul in the same chapter; "to love the life of the spirit is to think the thoughts of the spirit; and natural wisdom brings only death, whereas the wisdom of the spirit brings life and peace. That is because natural wisdom is at enmity with God, not submitting itself to his law; it is impossible that it should. Those who live the life of nature cannot be acceptable to God; but you live the life of the spirit, not the life of nature." This is surely the answer to those who would have it that Christian marriage is beyond them, that the Church's conditions are unreasonable, that the people[*] who lay down these principles have no idea of the circumstances in which married couples live, that nature makes its own laws, and has to be obeyed. "Nature has no longer any claim upon us," St. Paul goes on, "that we should live a life of nature." And, more strikingly still, a few verses further on: "created nature has been condemned to frustration." The frustration here is no idle sterility; it is rather a confinement which precedes a spiritual birth. Natural union gives place to the sacrament of matrimony.

From what has been said in the foregoing essay it might be supposed that the burden of guilt in unhappy marriages lies with the woman, and that the poor unfortunate male is always the victim (the ready victim, but the victim nevertheless) of the woman's wiles. As a corrective to this it must be said that if it is the woman who can all too frequently sell the pass, it is the man who can all too frequently buy it at any price. If flirtatiousness is the folly of the woman, precipitousness is the folly of the man. It is the man who sweeps the love along the channel of his own choosing, he who sets the pace. It is he who, whether from muddleheadedness or from malice, confuses the affectionate with the sensual — and who makes capital out of his mistake. This time it is Adam who trades on the generosity of Eve: he takes her apple at his own terms of valuation, not at hers — and often discovers it to be sour. Men are so blind: they will not see that by presuming and

---

[*] Like myself.

by grabbing — just as much as by wanting to have all the trees in the garden — they forfeit the one good thing to which they are entitled.

If it is through their good qualities that people are often found to fall, it is probably through the woman's superior instinct regarding sacrifice that she gives in too readily to the man she loves. To her the idea of self-giving comes more naturally than to the man: it is the appropriate expression of her devotion. This is why men are sometimes surprised to find women who are apparently good, who may even be married to someone else, surrendering themselves so easily: it is simply that they want to give everything. Sacrifice is the seal of love — even if it means the sacrifice of what has no right to be sacrificed and if the love is not worthy to be called love. To the woman this vision of sacrifice is sometimes so clear that it blots out everything else.

Again it might appear that with so vivid an idea of self-giving before her, the woman should stand a better chance of finding happiness in her love than does the man. Not necessarily. Certainly if the single act of sacrifice were the beginning and end of the whole thing, women would have the advantage over men. There is however this tendency in women, that, having given, they want more and more in return. Here is a new aspect of marriage's problem. The question now for her is how to temper the desire for demonstrative affection, for information, for reassurances; and for him it is a question of being infinitely patient and understanding.

Thus there comes a state in most marriages when, through a wife's thirst for a return of sacrifice, the husband's love can be turned into loathing, and when, through a husband's indifference, the wife's whole existence can be turned into a misery. On the one hand you have the wife unable to see how it is that she can give so much and he so little; on the other you have the husband unable to see why she must go on demanding what he feels he can no longer give. It is when these corresponding weaknesses are no longer covered up and allowed for, but are harped upon with resentment, that there is very great need for trust. It is a test time. The wife is being tempted to suspect her husband's love, to be jealous, to be self-pitying, to be alternately over-anxious to please and again bitterly reproachful; the husband is being tempted to find consolation away from home, to be cynical, to be deliberately wounding. If there is one thing a man cannot abide it is the sight of an abject, plaintive, martyred expression on a face he has vowed himself to live with for the rest of his life. Men, more easily exasperated by mute reproach than women, do not wear well in the continued presence of another's sorrow. This is especially the case when they feel that they are largely responsible for it: there is an evil streak in our natures which makes us determined to dislike the people we have wronged. One would have thought it would be the other way about, and that we would feel tender towards the victims of what afterwards we have come to recognise as our moods and our injustice, but it is not so: we harden our hearts against them and are more unjust than ever.

To conclude. Women should realise that they are never further from a man's pity than when they ask for it. They must know by faith if not by personal experience how disagreeable to a man is the idea of anyone exposing an injured heart; they must learn to stifle the note of appeal and above all how not to look pathetic. (This is not being untrue to one's real self; rather it is not giving way to one's weaker self. It is not so much adopting a disguise as effecting a suppression. Where the feebler side of our nature is concerned it is no virtue to be true: there is far more truth in practising a virtue which we haven't got than in yielding to a weakness which we have.) Men on the other hand should be prepared to meet their wives more than half-way; they should realise that, though the devotion which love claims from each is the same in essence, it is different in expression, and that what to the male mind is either trivial or assumed is to the feminine mind both significant and crying out for demonstration. On each side, the man's and the woman's, there is therefore the paramount need of understanding — particularly that brand of it which goes on with the act of trust and the will to sympathise when misunderstanding charges the air. This is the only solution known to man for meeting the marriage problem.

# THE MARRIAGE IDEAL

**I**T HAS BEEN TRULY POINTED out[*] that marriage is rated so high in God's sight that the terms used by Him for calling souls to it are almost identical with those by which He invites to His discipleship: just as a man may leave mother, father, brothers and sisters in order to follow Him, so for the cause of matrimony he may do the same. This is vastly important: it means that discipleship and marriage share similar privileges, similar obligations, similar ideals and similar consequences. As regards the consequences it means that where the purpose of either vocation is defeated, there can only be unhappiness and disaster. Thus the soul who, having accepted the call either to religion or to the state of matrimony, makes a mess of it, is worse off than if he had never been called at all: his response sets the seal to the sacredness of his obligation. The married man, no less than the monk, must know the quality of his responsibility. He is not only responsible to his wife and to his children—as the religious is not only responsible to his superior and to his community—he is responsible, directly, to God. For a married man

---

[*] By a number of people — each of them assuming originality.

or woman to live in a state of accepted infidelity, to indulge in contraceptive practices, to procure certain birth-eliminating treatments or to make use of the State's way out when the marriage has come to be an acknowledged failure would be so to reverse the order set by God that not only would it have been better to have remained single but it would have been better not to have shared in humanity's privileges at all. If man is going to live by his passions he might just as well be an animal. Better be an animal in fact, because if an animal were to violate the natural law there would at least be nothing morally wrong about it. Marriage laws are not drawn up by God and the Church in order to make matters more difficult for man; they express what is already in man as God made him, and so direct his natural instincts in a way which will make happiness more easy for him. If the animal passions are allowed to dominate in marriage, happiness is impossible. Christian ideals, with their necessary laws, are there to control passion and to lay down conditions for happiness.

We have seen that the dignity of marriage has a more than casual resemblance to the dignity of the religious vocation. All things being equal, the celibate life, undertaken for the love of God, is a higher estate than the married life. But there is no merit in being single as such. The married state is very much higher, objectively, than that of the bachelor or the spinster: it is under the cover of special sacramental graces, it has its vows, it is a sanctifying state, it is a vocation. Where the single individual has only himself or herself to worry about, the partners in marriage have each other and their children to consider. The wear and tear are shared as in a religious community, the sacrifice becomes corporate, the resources are pooled, there is no isolationist enjoyment of its fruits, the delights and disappointments of the part are the delights and disappointments of the whole. Such, at all events, is the ideal. It is an ideal which calls for great generosity and a constant willingness to subdue selfish interest. But then that is what the partners in marriage took on. That is why they were allowed to fall in love — so that they might have sufficient spirit to offer themselves for the work. They have loved, they have offered, and now they see where their generosity has led them. For the rest of their lives it will mean infinite patience, infinite trust, infinite hope. Do they want to go back on it all merely because they have been taken at their word? Merely because they are being held to playing the heroic part which was so readily theirs in anticipation? They must remember that at every moment the grace is present to sustain them in whatever heroisms they may be called upon to practise.

The marriage ideal, then, is no mere academic theory; it is a practical reality. Its implications are expected of ordinary Christians. Dependent neither upon the early emotional attraction nor upon a code of purely preventative laws, Christian marriages are kept together by the combined effect of grace, mutual fidelity, trust. The sanctity of marriage is not a negative thing, forbidding transgression; it is a positive one, putting power into the hands of men and women and safeguarding the happiness of both of them. Even the restraint which they exercise in their relations together is not prohibitive so much as creative: her modesty and his gentleness combine to form a protective screen which allows the right ordering of their joint creative act. Without this shelter the act, right in itself originally by nature and made more than right by the grace of the sacrament conferred by Christ and His Church, is exposed to evil from within and without. Sins against the sacrament of matrimony are sins against God, against the soul committing them, against the partner in marriage, and against the unborn child. The sacrament of the Holy Eucharist is not the only sacrament which is Blessed; the Body of Christ is not the only body to be held sacred. We are limbs of Christ's body, says St. Paul to the Ephesians; flesh and bone we belong to Him. "Do not allow anyone to cheat you with empty promises ... as for the thankless deeds which men do in the dark, you must not take any part in them ... it is the light that rebukes such things and shows them up for what they are ... see then how carefully you have to walk, not as fools but as wise men do.... No, you cannot afford to be reckless; you must grasp what is the Lord's will for you."

To the Corinthians the apostle is even more explicit. "Surely you know that your bodies are the shrines of the Holy Spirit who dwells in you . . . you are no longer your own masters. A great price was paid for your ransom; glorify God by making your bodies the shrines of his presence."[*]

---

[*] See also the verses shortly before: namely, 1 Corinthians vi. 15-19.

# THE IDEAL MARRIAGE

HOUGH NO ONE NEED BE accused of cynicism who concludes after looking about him that the ideal marriage is the rarest thing in the world, most on the other hand would admit that quite a number of reasonably happy married couples are to be found, and that families do exist where harmony, security, and fun generally, seem to flourish. Hitherto in these sections on the married life we have been considering particularly the relations between husband and wife; the present section has to do specifically with the family. In view of the purpose of marriage, the ideal can hardly be realised without the existence of the children.

It is perhaps not universally recognised that the last hundred years have witnessed a conjugal revolution every bit as far-reaching in its consequences as the industrial revolution. At no period in the history of man have the three supports of the family—namely the fidelity of husband and wife, the indissoluble character of the marriage bond, and the fecundity of the union—been so seriously menaced. This is the direct and inevitable consequence of easy divorce: wherever it has been found possible to loosen the ties which people have wound around their lives in the days of their early love, the opportunities have been taken advantage of, and the results have been disastrous for the community. Marital integrity has come to be thought of as the exception rather than the norm, unions are not even embarked upon with the same idea of their permanence, and where sixty years ago the average number of children in a family was seven it is now rather less than two. When man begins to tamper with the law of God in any direction he cannot but be laying up trouble for himself in the long run; nowhere is this more clearly shown than when he tampers with the law of God regarding marriage. By this time man should know that by readily separating what God has joined together he is saddling the world with three definitely recognisable evils: promiscuity, a breaking up of the home life, and a lowering of the birthrate.

God designed the family as a unit founded upon the lifelong union of man and woman. Parenthood does not begin and end with the act of procreation. Nor can there be any such things as filial affection, obedience to parental authority, development of family happiness, where the conditions of the so-called home are non-conjugal and impermanent. The charter which God has laid down for marriage rejects all thought of polygamy and polyandry; the State leaves the door open for both. Where there is this conflict of view, and where man takes it upon himself to interpret the law according to his own view, there is bound to be trouble. Man has to pay in the end, and he is paying for it now: the foundations of education, of national spirit, of moral and intellectual and even physical well-being are suffering.*

Neither the ingenuity of politicians nor the discoveries of science can find an adequate substitute for the begetting and bringing up of children by parents united in wedlock. Experiments in artificial insemination, communal nurseries, and indeed in any direction which leads away from the natural rights which spring from the home, are doomed to failure. It is difficult to see how a country like our own which has so far departed from Christian standards as, for instance, to cater for promiscuity in the services can ever regain its moral balance. A miracle of grace could reverse the general tendency, but nothing much else could. In societies where the family is so little respected and safeguarded as it is in ours, history has invariably repeated itself in its record of decline. The process is uniform: take away the authority of the parents — *auctoritas*, the prerogative of the *auctor*, the increaser — and respect for the law, respect for the dignity and power of the

---

\* The State, needless to say, has not been slow to observe these drifts. The State has accordingly stepped in and assumed many of the rights which belong by nature to the family. More and more the control is being handed over by the dwindling family to the developing State. In matters of education, care of the sick, housing, insurance and pensions — all at one time the province of the individual and the home — the State claims to have the deciding voice. Of course — because the family has no voice left.

State, goes with it. Take away the sanctity of marriage, and the springs of freedom, of pride in property and posterity, of love for tradition are broken. It is one of the paradoxes of human nature that selfishness, whether personal or national, destroys its own ends: when a man has nobody else to work for or fight for except himself, he loses interest. A man may work in order to keep himself alive, and fight in order to save his skin, but there is all the difference between what is done for necessity and what is done for a cause. Remove the family as a cause and the results will very soon show the harmful effects of compulsion.

"This is all very depressing," you will say, "but I don't see that there is anything to be done about it." Granted that the private individual has little opportunity of putting across his Christian principles from the platform, there is surely scope for him in the unit which we have been considering — namely the family. Every man and woman can see to it that at least in *this* home the remedies may be applied and the ideal marriage secured. Surely it is not too much to expect of a Catholic household — or even of one Catholic in a non-Catholic but predominantly Christian household — to stand strictly for such things as decency and modesty (how old-fashioned the word "modesty" already sounds — evidence again of the modern drift away from Christian standards), for the right use of the marriage act, for mutual fidelity, for the permanence of marriage as an institution and for its inherent sanctity as a sacrament, for the moral obligation of self-sacrifice, for the responsibility of spiritual as well as temporal assistance, for the religious upbringing of the children, and for the necessity of prayer in the general life of the whole. If these aspects of matrimony are treated lightly or neglected altogether it is not to be wondered at that the ideal marriage has yet to be discovered. For those who complain that their marriage has been a failure the Church provides a clear-cut examination of conscience.

# *THE STATE AND THE SOUL*

HAT WE TEND TO FORGET is that States are people. States are not houses of parliament or legislative measures or international congresses: they are human souls with a plan. Often the plan is the wrong one, and often the human souls are concerned more with material than spiritual ends, but so far as final purpose goes, the State's is the same as that of the individual and of the family.

The ideal State is the large-scale family; the family is people. People come before States. States derive their origin and their authority through the people whom they rule — and so through families. The right to rule is from God — but it comes through people. The first society is the family, not the State. The family is the perfect society in miniature; the State is (at best) the perfect family magnified. If every family were self-dependent, there would be no State: there would only be country, or town, or district. But because families, in order to exist and develop, have to come to one another's assistance there have to be States. The State is therefore the consequence, not the cause, of man's social nature. But, as so often happens in the affairs of mankind, the effect tends to develop at the expense of the cause: the State gradually begins to assume the rights of the family, overruling its original authority and even, sometimes, turning against its original purpose. So soon as a State proposes some end of its own, neglecting the well-being of its constituent elements or not listening to their claims in self-development, it reverses God's purpose and is unworthy of governing. This rules out Totalitarian States at once.

Thus, if States go wrong, morally, when they pursue a policy which is independent of the persons in it, statesmen go wrong, morally, when they subscribe to the party programme overriding the individual need. That men in responsible positions should do this must sound very wicked indeed. Yet they are doing it every day—and in so-called Christian countries. With their eyes open, but seeing only the good of the whole or the fulfilment of the theory, statesmen and politicians are waiving away the inalienable rights of the single unit. This may seem very wicked, but it should hardly seem very surprising: where no search is made for what is outside the present life, it is the inevitable consequence. Where the supernatural destiny of mankind is ignored, the natural rights which were designed towards the attainment of this end find no support.

Politics are intended to be the means of realising ethical principles. Such, anyway, was the original plan. Politics are meant to open the door to what theology and philosophy decide upon as a code of right behaviour. "This is the good life," says the thinker; "it leads to happiness and to God." "Very well," says the politician; "we must adopt it and extend it for the benefit of all." The assumption here is that the thinker is a Christian moralist, and the politician an honest man. It is a bold assumption.

That politics have gone off the Christian standard is all too evident. In fact, having slid away from the ethics of the Gospel, politics now excuse themselves from observing any sort of ethics at all. At one time morality was not a private duty as it is now; it was a public standard. Public and home affairs were integrated; there was a unity. Today there is no such reflex check-up: whatever people do in their own houses as regards social relations is their affair; politics, whether national or international, are run on a basis of expediency. Religion, for example, may not enter into questions of public policy. "It isn't the slightest use applying evangelical principles in our dealings with those who are opposed to us," says the politician; "we wouldn't be understood." And the awful part of it is that this is true. Once one side refuses to play, all the others begin to cheat. What used to be at least a recognition of the spiritual realities has been replaced by exclusively material considerations. The only things which count for anything in international relations are power and threat and bribe. The idea of trust between nations is laughable.[*]

---

[*] Yet the present Pope has been insisting that nations cannot hope to solve their problems until they begin to trust one another.

Children growing up in the modern world may be excused if they imagine that patriotism's finest expression is the savage bravery of the hater. For them diplomacy is nothing more than the ability to outwit an opposite number by underhand means. Eventually it must come to this, that a nation's well-being is assessed by the degree to which it has been able to eliminate its rivals, whether in trade or in the field. It is the ugly story of the master race, the Herrenvolk. In a world where peace is maintained only by the balance of fear, where finance takes sharp practice for granted, where ideals in matters of sex are looked upon as a survival from the mistaken ages of piety, there is little room for the Christian conscience. No account is taken of the soul who is disgusted by the non-Christian and amoral evidences which appear in contemporary legislation, in art and literature, in the tolerance extended to such things as nudism and its literature, to salacious films, to plays and even broadcasts which are not only tendentious but positively subversive. How — to return again to the family which is after all the heart of the matter — can young people learn to take their place in society if the idea of government looms larger than the idea of father and mother, if laws are conceived of as disciplines to be evaded, if money is taken as the final end and test of success, if happiness is identified with pleasures which can be bought, if love is seen as a thing of the senses, if religion is judged to be a suitable interest for those who have a taste for it? The way of life which modern civilisation has adopted makes no allowance for the yearning of the soul. How can it? By relegating it to the sacristy it has virtually denied the existence of the soul.

Politics cannot be held entirely responsible — any more than the cinema or the economic state of mankind or the two wars can be held responsible — for the alienation of man from his spiritual inheritance, but it is indisputable that if politics took Christianity as a basis there would be a return to natural relations between societies, classes, and peoples. In order to achieve this return, governments would have to plan in a Christian way, would have to *think* Christianity, would even have to practise it in their private lives. Governments, again, are individuals. Governments are — let us face it — *ourselves*. The State is our concern as much as it is the concern of politicians. If in the Body of Christ one member must supply what the other lacks, then we so-called religious people must pray our way, Christ's way, into the parliaments of the world. This does not necessarily mean that religiously minded men and women must force themselves to take an interest in politics: it means that politically minded men and women — indeed *all* men and women — must force themselves to take an interest in religion.

# *AS WITH NATIONS SO WITH PEOPLE*

WHAT HAPPENS TO A COUNtry in a century may happen to an individual in less than a decade. Without ever going to the length of formal apostasy, a man may, every bit as fatally as a nation, allow false standards to replace true ones. Often the process of deterioration is exactly the same as that observed above in the case of the State: material cares crowd out the needs of the spirit, quick returns are demanded without regard to ultimate ends. In some cases, while the life of the soul is being whittled down to nothing at all, there is no great sense of guilt or loss. Gradual substitutions evoke no emotion either way—there is neither remorse nor self-congratulation. As in the case of the nation, the individual wakes up to find himself pagan—and then goes to sleep again.

In those periods of history when States have gone pagan there was all the more need for the individual members of them to go spiritual. There is exactly this need today. How else, except by the sanctifying of the parts, can spiritual health be restored to the whole? The parts must know where they stand as regards such fundamentals as religion and happiness before the whole, as represented by a government, can be brought to recognise their claims. In a recent Gallup Poll on the subject of happiness, only three per cent mentioned religion has having anything at all to do with it. Where a Catholic tradition assumes the essential connexion between the two, the modern interpretation of life sees only an accidental one — if that.

All this is only another presentation of the old struggle between the world of the senses and the world of the spirit. The man who refuses to live the life of faith, refuses to pray, becomes so caught up in outward things that supernatural claims are simply not seen — much less bothered about. Religion restates man's purpose, readjusts his values, redirects his energies, and by so enlarging his vision and capacity enables him to pick up his happiness and put it in its proper place. Religion and happiness, though not necessarily cause and effect, are to this extent connected — that the truly religious man knows where to look for his happiness, and the truly happy man knows that his conscience plays a far more important part in contributing to his wellbeing than does anything outside himself.

In this way happiness and unhappiness are not seen as things in themselves, as squared-off blocks of experience which are to be labelled either reward or punishment, but rather as habits of mind which emerge from one or other orientation. Being able to arrange one's outward life as one wants it is no more a guarantee of happiness than the failure to do so need necessarily spell unhappiness. The mind must find something more solid than plans for present security to lean on. Man may not live on bread alone. He needs faith. This involves, for most of us, considerable discipline: it probably means that we have to re-set the order of our appetites, attaching new values as we go along.

If the primary mistake is to see happiness in terms of pleasurable excitement, then the first step towards wisdom is to examine the possibility of happiness existing in the midst of dullness. Experience shows that it can, and that mere monotony has nothing to do with happiness. Happiness is not put off by the commonplace; it rather likes it. Real happiness is independent even of downright drudgery. You can be perfectly happy doing dull and even unagreeable things — which can be proved by the way in which you do not in the least mind doing thoroughly boring things when you happen to be in particularly good form or if you are doing them with someone you are fond of. Essential dullness does not depend upon the thing at all: occupations which are objectively dull need not be so to the person — are not so to the happy person. Occupations in themselves boring, then, do not affect happiness: the way you look at boring occupations does.

If happiness is independent of dullness, it is certainly independent of sensation. Entertainment has about as little to do with happiness as the first frenzied infatuation has to do with love: both can be symptoms or expressions or indications of the underlying quality, but they are not the last word on it. Indeed these two sentiments, happiness and love, bear one another out in the present investigation. For instance, you do not have to look for entertainment when you are in love: it is there whether you think of it or not. You do not, when in that state, have to escape from the dull things. On the contrary you find, because of the other person's presence (either actual or in the mind) a certain satisfaction in doing them. The satisfaction overrides the sensation. The things which you do when you are happy — as when you are in love — are, leaving aside the moral issue for the moment, immaterial. So far as your happiness goes, they minister to your pleasure; they are, whatever you may feel about them when you are not in a state of happiness, so many evidences of your joy. It means that you are taking up outside life and enjoying it; outside life is being assimilated into the happiness within.

In conclusion. By reversing the Gospel exhortation to "Seek first the kingdom of God, and all these things shall be added to you" the world cuts off its face to spite its nose. As with nations, so with individuals. Thus it is for us, in an atmosphere of non-comprehension, to hold out uncompromisingly on not only the absolute values but also the relative elements in man's fulfilment. The kingdom of God has the paramount claim, and all these things which are added we receive as coming from Him.

# ENVY AND
# ITS OPPOSITE

"IF YOU WANT TO KNOW WHAT envy is," said Disraeli rather unkindly, "you should live among artists." Disraeli never lived among artists himself, and so may be excused for mistaking something else in the artist for the vice which he so much disliked. (Though it is curious to note in passing that Disraeli was not able to find what he wanted among politicians.) Certainly one artist seldom admires the work of another artist, but this need not be due to envy, crude and simple. Ideally every artist should admire every other artist— seeing in a different interpretation the complement of his own, seeing the development of a parallel purpose, the birth of a new expression to the same concept, a reflexion of beauty which opens windows on horizons not glimpsed before—but in fact he does not. As a rule the reason for this is not that one man is grudging success to another, but that both have visions of beauty so individual that neither can get the angle of the other's. Oscar Wilde (who *did* live among artists) says that in art only the mediocre are mutually admiring. If this is true it is because the mediocre have not the single eye of the masters. The only artist who can perfectly and wholeheartedly admire the creative expression of others is the artist in sanctity. Which brings us to the point of this chapter: we are discussing the saint's approach to life—which is at once the most sensible, the most rewarding, the most realist, and the most artistic.

Envy is impossible to the saint, because saints enter into the minds of others. The saint does not look at another man's work and say: "I would have done it differently." He does not consider whether it is done better or worse than he would have done it; he simply considers it as an outward indication of another man's mind and as such worthy of respect. Which is why the saint jumps for joy when he sees sincerity: it makes it so much easier for him to enter into the mind of the other. True, the saint may not like it when he gets there, but on the other hand he is not trying to live in other people's heads for his own amusement.

The saint, accepting as true the dictum that the artist's imagination must operate in the world, whether factual or fantastic, that is most natural to it, seeks in literature, painting, music and the drama, for a beauty which someone else has either expressed or revealed before him. That is to say, his one idea is not originality; he is not keen to be hailed a pioneer, the founder of a school, the inspiration of a movement. He wants to uncover more and more of the truth as he sees it, but he knows very well that the truth is there all the time and that if he doesn't uncover it somebody else will. The saint is quite happy to get along with the truth which is already revealed; he is even a little bit afraid of trying his hand at the work of uncovering more in case he should find himself drawing attention to his own handiwork instead of to truth and beauty. He prefers, unless he is pushed by Providence, to leave it to others. God can use whatever means He likes, *when* He likes, in the work of revealing more of Himself to man. "All I have to see to," says the saint, "is that I am neither so lazy as to do nothing, or so up-and-coming as to be an exhibitionist. The best thing for me is to learn from other men's work." There is not much room for envy here.

The starting point for the saint is different from that of the critic or competitor. The saint is never on the level which gives him the desire to look down and pick holes; he is always much more ready to look up and assume that there are no holes to pick. It is not for him to go one better; all he wants is to learn from others how he can better be himself. In searching for truth a man finds both himself and other people. The discovery may be unconscious at the time, but it amounts to the gift of understanding in the long run: it is the habit of sympathy.

Though the saint, in assuming the best instead of the worst of other people, may err on the score of strict outward accuracy, he is a realist nevertheless: he sees, with God, what they were really made for and what they are really capable of being. He sees the soul in its constituent elements rather than what the outward man has made of the outward opportunity. Seeing the fact of God's love for every individual soul, he sees men as potentially responsive to the influence of grace. Which is what they are. So he is a realist. The mystic is always nearer to the truth, if he is a true mystic, than is the materialist. Most of us are so far from the mystic vision as hardly to qualify as realists at all. We live on illusions of one kind and another, and are afraid to know the truth. Reality shocks us, so we see to it that films of unreality veil our eyes. Not so the saint: for him there does not exist the same fear of looking at life as it really is; he has no need to create a dream world for himself before he can be happy. He is at his happiest with truth.

For us, whose lives are so thickly larded with either settled prejudice or delusion in good faith (or simply with sheer matter), it is not easy to recognise truth when we see it — let alone be true to what it shows us. We do not give ourselves the chance. If individuals act inconsistently not only with their purpose as human beings but with their particularly selected natures as individuals, they can hardly expect to retain the innocent eye of the saint and mystic. Consistency is the secret of being able to see straight; only the integrated man, the balanced and unified man, can get his focus right on life. But about this subject of integrity there will be a certain amount to be said in a section of its own. Suffice it here to note that the only man who is really proof against the ramifications of envy is the man who is so poised within that he has no need to worry about competition without. Not that he is self-sufficient, but that his sufficiency comes from God.

# THE OTHER ENVY

THE CATECHISM WARNS US against the envy of another's spiritual good, and of all the sins open to man this is probably the least popular. For one thing, since the temptation is supposedly felt only by the devout, the majority are not even aware of its occasions; for another, there are so many more attractive things to be jealous about than our neighbour's progress in the ways of the spirit that the average Christian does not bother. But though rare *in that particular form*—namely of grudging another his higher place than ours on the ladder of perfection—it is very common indeed in another. While we may not envy our neighbour's spiritual good, we very often envy the spiritual good which we imagine that we ourselves would be enjoying if things were slightly different from what they are.

Many in religion as well as in the world are constantly complaining that with another set of natural advantages — or with a rearrangement of the set which they have got — they could serve God much better than they do, and at the same time be far happier. "Given better health (or better brains, or better looks, or more money, or a more congenial environment, or more understanding people to work for) I could have been a success by this time . . . whereas, things being as they are, I am spiritually and temporally a failure." In a sense this is to envy another's spiritual (and temporal) good. It is to envy the good of another self. It is all the more idle because the other self does not happen, as things are, to exist.

If individual souls are created singly, and at the same time in relation to the general plan, there cannot be anything haphazard about the allocation of qualities: every gift, every limitation, every potentiality must be exactly measured to the particular requirements of every particular individual. There is nothing fatalistic about this; it is, given a belief in man's supernatural origin and destiny, stark common sense. How could it be otherwise? No all-wise Creator can be thought of as launching His creatures upon a certain part of the world's surface and at a certain point in the world's history, while simultaneously endowing them with talents and interests which would have suited them splendidly somewhere else or if they had been living in a different generation, but which, in existing circumstances, are entirely useless. The parable of the talents has negative as well as positive implications: if we are meant on the one side to make use of the talents which we have got and not to worry about the ones which we would like, we are meant on the other to accept our disadvantages as they are and not to worry about what we would be like, or be able to do, without them. We know all this; we have been told it innumerable times; the term "God's will," which we use so frequently, covers precisely such situations. But the wistful refrain (no, it is worse than that—it is a pitiable whine) goes on and on and on and on before the throne of God: "If only, Lord, I hadn't been born with this inherited temperament . . . if only I'd had a better education . . . if only I didn't feel so tired all the time . . . if only I were twenty years younger . . . if only I could be given another job . . . if only the right sort of treatment . . . a different part of the country . . . never had a proper chance . . . " And so it goes on.

So-called accidents of birth such as have been mentioned, are not accidents, but ingredients: they do not diminish our chances but add to them. If any of these conditions which we complain are lacking to us would have increased our chances of happiness or holiness, we may depend upon it that the fact would not have escaped Almighty God.*

---

* Let me here introduce the only personal reflexion which will be found in this book, and say that having been ill for most of my life and ugly for all of it, I am fully convinced that these factors have been of enormous advantage to me. We do not see these things at the time, and even looking back they are sometimes not as clear as they might be. All I can say is that had I in my case been well all my life I would not have read or prayed or left myself in God's hands, and had I been better-looking I would not have escaped the situations in which the more handsome of my friends seem constantly to be getting themselves involved. (Not, I hasten to add, that I wouldn't have been a good deal happier and able to do more for God if my lot had been cast where there was more sun. If only I had started off in California or the South Sea Islands, instead of having to contend with this miserable climate of ours, there's no knowing what I mightn't, etc. etc. etc.)

This is not to claim that you can, by the simple process of adjusting your mind with a click to the existing order of things, be just as happy in a concentration camp as on a cruise in the Mediterranean or while ski-ing at St. Moritz. The theory covers the setting of life, not the interludes. It means that, taking the over-all view, you don't have to consider the possibilities of any other state but that in which you are placed. If the concentration camp (or the cruise) is a permanent affair, then the situation is altered: it is covered by the particular vocational grace which is proper to the life. All you have to do then is to find the perfect concentration camp existence — and it is unreasonable to believe that God will not make this possible.

Thus the answer to that particular kind of disgruntlement which comes of envying a non-existent self who is living under hypothetical circumstances is again — as it was in the case of the other, more obvious, envy — fidelity to the truth. The scholastic axiom "live according to what you are, and you will grow" is all-embracing. According to what you are, not according to what you are not. The whole thing depends on consistency. Which is truth. There is no other secret — either of happiness or holiness.

# VOCATIONAL GRACE

HEN BLESSED CLAUDE DE la Colombière says that "neglect of the duties of their state of life is the commonest sin among pious people," he is making what at first sight seems a very obvious remark. But surely he does not mean only that devout people are tempted to be slack when the novelty of their vocation is beginning to wear off (as if there were few other opportunities open to them in the way of sin), but rather that pious people are often so anxious to be good in all directions that the particular good which has been placed by God in their direction is overlooked. Following what has been said in the two foregoing essays, this is the place to consider the question of specific graces attaching to specific calls.

"Thus shall my word be that shall go forth from my mouth," says the Lord in the prophecy of Isaias, "and it shall not return to me void." There is here the idea of grace circulating through the universe and coming back again to its source. It is as if every syllable of God's utterance, no sooner fallen from His lips, is caught up on the great wheel of grace and carried round in the unceasing sweep of what is at once God's munificence and man's opportunity. There, at some inalienable point on the circumference, stands every soul whom God has made: each with his chance of either responding or letting the word go by. What happens if the word gets back to God — void?

God's gifts are lent to us; they are not ours to do what we like with. If we are careless and do not read the directions on the box, or, having read them, either decide that we know better or else make use of the gift in our way instead of in His, we are sending God's word spinning back to Him *void*. We shall, moreover, not only be wasting an opportunity but we shall be in fact worse off than if we had never received the gift at all. Every gift has its own responsibilities, its own directions, its own problems. The trouble begins when, granted that we have accepted it, we start interpreting its use. The gift is always the apt gift — as we have seen above — and the Giver is always there to show us how to use it; it is we who turn it to our condemnation. There is nothing wrong with a sword, but if we take it up in the wrong way we perish by it. God's gifts are two-edged. Christ Himself was set for the fall and resurrection of many — Christ who gave Himself to man, Christ the supreme gift. The thought is echoed by St. Paul when he tells the Corinthians that "he who eateth and drinketh unworthily, eateth and drinketh judgement to himself." Of all God's graces may it be said, as Isaias said of the Messias, that they are "a stumbling block and a rock of scandal, and whosoever believeth shall not be confounded."

Thus each man's state of life, though ordered towards his sanctification, is more likely to cause his downfall if he neglects the particular graces attaching to it than any stray evil which he may come across outside that state of life. Accordingly the religious of an active order finds or loses his vocation in activity, the contemplation in hiddenness. The temptation of the preacher is in his pulpit, of the thinker in his thought. The holier the work, the greater the evil which shadows it. It is that which might have been the greatest blessing which can turn out the most effective as a curse. Isaias and Blessed Claude say the same thing. The call that has gone forth from God may not return to Him an empty echo; and if we do not take the note as it passes, it will come back to us on the next round as a reproach. Vocational grace, misused, is its own liability. It was in the character of an apostle that Judas sinned. Who would have worried about Lucifer if he had not been an archangel?

Here is a parable. There was once a man who lived near a zoo. He had retired earlier than he need have done from his business so as to be able to look forward to a good long time with his wife and children. The home was a very happy one, and each evening the whole family would go round to the zoo together and spend a delightful hour throwing little bits of things to their favourites among the animals. The man was so sympathetically inclined towards every kind of bird and beast — even the wildest of them became tame the moment he arrived at their cages — that the superintendent of the zoo, noticing this, asked him one day if he would accept employment as a sort of glorified keeper. "Who, me?" said the man. "Oh no, I've retired. I've got my own greedy and chattering family to look after at home." He said this with a gay ugh because it struck him as mildly funny to imply that the zoo was a sort of family. "Besides," he added, "it would be no fun if I *had* to do it." But as time went on and the man spent more and more time with the animals, less and less with his wife and children, the nice superintendent came to him again and suggested, with much more persuasiveness this time, that though there need be no question of a uniform or a salary or anything like that, it would be doing the zoo a great favour if he, the man, would come and live over among the animals who were so devoted to him. They would then be able to have him in and out at odd times, just whenever he chose. "To see the little fellows perched on your shoulder and running up and down your front," said the genial superintendent (an infant monkey was feeling for ginger biscuits in the man's waistcoat pocket at the time), "is a cheering sight to old eyes. Think of the good you could do if you came and joined us permanently." Well in the end the man, who had, as they said, "such a way with animals," was too kindhearted to refuse: he was installed in a pretty little lodge quite close to the ostriches. His wife and family missed him very much at home (because for some reason they were unable to live within the enclosure — perhaps the lodge was too small or there may have been rules about going out and coming in after dark). They began to give up their evening visits to the various cages because it was no fun any more: what they had enjoyed was going all together. They went to the cinema instead — in ones and twos. Eventually, to bring this sad story to a close, the superintendent died and the man whose fortunes we have been considering, was chosen, with no hesitation on anybody's part, to take his place. You will not be surprised to hear that he lived to become the most famous and respected superintendent that the zoo had ever had — beloved by all, staff and animals alike.[*] And at home his wife was constantly being told "how lucky you are to be married to such a nice important husband who is so good with animals."

This story suits any of the last few chapters — and probably one or two more which are yet to come.

---

[*] On alternate Wednesdays, when the zoo was closed to visitors, he used to take his children to somewhere amusing for tea. But he was always back by feeding time.

# THE SCHIZOPHRENIC AGE

INCE IT IS THE FASHION TO label the times in which we live, referring cheerfully to the Atomic Age and the Age of Dictators and the Totalitarian Age, we might do worse than borrow a label from the psychologists. The schizophrenic age. Though the nature of man has always been self-contradictory—a fact which has accounted for his moral struggle since the fall of Adam—it is not until today that his inconsistencies have been so scientifically sorted out. Whether it does him any good or not to see the complexities of his multiple character spread out and pinned down to a cork remains to be seen; psycho-analysis has not been going long enough to justify itself.

According to present opinion it is men who are by nature more inconsistent than women. One wonders (as a complete outsider and with no professional knowledge) whether this conclusion may not be based on the way men behave, rather than upon the way they are made. It seems at least probable that men and women are equally liable to these divergencies in their temperament, but that men, being more escapist than women, show it more. Women too are escapist, but with them it takes the less obvious form of self-deception.

Where a woman, afraid to face her real self, creates a part to play and keeps it up so well that eventually she hardly knows the difference between her real and imaginary self, a man, just as unwilling to face his real self, goes out and tries to forget about it. Where the one escapes into the imagination, the other escapes into satisfaction. If, as Kipling concluded, the female of the species is the more deadly, she is also the more deep. Both male and female run away from the loneliness of their failure; the difference is that the male runs into the open and looks for compensations and distractions which he knows in his heart of hearts are not the expressions of his real self at all but of his fear; while the female runs underground — and so eludes the psychologists. The reason why men take to drink and indulge the appetites generally is not because they are fundamentally more vicious but because they cannot stand the loneliness which is by-passed more effectively in other ways by the majority of women.

It is not a black mood or a sudden impulse which makes good people do bad things; nor is it a flash of generosity which makes bad people do good ones. It is simply the settled longing to get away from self. We all, men and women alike, come to realise before very long that there is a flaw within ourselves, a blight which lies upon our every good, so, rather than look at it and be faced with the ceaseless struggle to keep it under, we try and carry one self outside into the sun and leave the other indoors to manage on its own. Literature is full of this conflict, full of characters who are at enmity with themselves and who break out. The outcasts of Conrad and Graham Greene, the cowards of Mason and Benson, the misfits of Ibsen, Maurois, Dostoevsky, Stendahl and Tolstoy are all either disproving a part of their natures which they know exists or else hiding away from what they feel that God is wanting of them. The stifling of a religious vocation is only the reverse side of the same coin which tries to buy up lotus leaves. The sad thing is that once the decision to be dishonest with themselves has been made, people find that they are pledged to a course of subterfuge and substitution. It is our old friend the Ancient Mariner: shoot the albatross and out goes life on the ship.

The *Ballad of Reading Gaol* is true in that when man kills the thing he loves, he does so not because of a fit of hate but because of a dread of love. It is man's fatal tendency to decry what he has failed at. When man knows that he has fallen short of what love expected from him, he turns upon it. The libertine is seldom either a careless philanderer from the start or a sensualist by nature: more often than not he is a man who has spoiled his share of love, and is out to discredit love itself. The casual or cynical lover is trying to convince himself, by his squalid caricature of the thing, that love is no more than what the world makes it out to be. It is humbling to think that we should want to kill what we have maimed—and that we should want this simply to save ourselves the trouble of remembering and living with the memory—but it is nevertheless what we might expect. Love (or indeed any other good) becomes, when deflected, its own opposite. Sacrifice becomes selfishness, the spiritual becomes carnal, sweetness becomes bitter and savage and wrong.

What Wilde saw in its extreme, most of us see in its less stark and cruelly revealing form—or if we don't, it is because we refuse to look. Where perhaps only the minority of mankind may, with set teeth, destroy the things they love, most of us certainly take steps to disguise them. But to disguise and deny is to kill, is to abuse, is to turn the gift against itself. The world is suffering from having its goods turned into evils. This, more than any other, is our present misfortune—that our enemies are those of our own household, that the obstacles to our development are just those things which were designed to be our greatest help. The world, abusing the rights of men and women, has arrived at despising men and women. Man, by abusing love and marriage and the elemental things, has come to despise love and everything connected with it. "Don't preach to me about love. I know what it's for. Sordid but inescapable." This is the Manicheism of our times—that we refuse to see where our good things come from, and so, eventually, lower our estimate of their worth.

# SIN

HERE ARE TWO MISTAKES which people make about sin (apart from that of committing it), and though one seems more disastrous than the other, they equally paralyse the effort to overcome it. The first is the error of imagining that any one line of sin is a natural weakness for which the soul is not really responsible and which, given the appropriate treatment, can be cured in the ordinary way like a disease. The second is the folly of believing that sin kills both the soul's power to respond to grace and God's desire for the soul to respond. Where one man says that he is a special case and that God's law doesn't apply, the other says that he too is a special case and that God cannot possibly love anyone who has treated Him so badly. Both of them are acting on the assumption that God does not mean what He says, and that in any case they know better than the Church. The two heresies, in practice arriving at the same defeatism, are at opposite extremes in their attack upon hope. They will here be treated separately.

"I know that according to the text-book it may be wrong, but then the text-book lays down the law for the normal run of mankind. I happen to be one of the unfortunate exceptions, and I am sure God understands. He must know that I am made like this. So what I do now is to put it down to inherited weakness or split personality or a gap of some sort in my make-up, and just go ahead." If this means that there is no sorrow for guilt, no purpose of amendment, no petition for strength and pardon and light on the particular problem, then the non-recognition of personal responsibility is no excuse. It is an assumed dispensation to which no soul can possibly have a right. Very good reasons indeed would have to be advanced before a confessor could accept the view that any continued material sin was non-culpable. (And, even so, the confessor would look for better dispositions than those suggested above.)

The attitude of presumption with regard to sin is far more common now than it used to be. It is the psychologists who are responsible for this. Where a soul would be told by a moralist to fight his vicious tendencies, he is often advised by a psycho-analyst to let them have reasonable outlet. "You are unrealised," the so-called patient is told; "you have probably been inhibited from birth; what you want is a little experience so as to release the pressure." The tempted soul is informed that though there is bound to be a certain interior conflict, and though objectively good remains good, and evil remains evil, there must not be this sense of strain ... there must be a readjustment in the matter of right and wrong ... it is the subjective angle that must decide it. The result of this is that the man lets himself go, and the tendency is accepted as being a semi-pathological appetite for which he need be no longer accountable.

Even if the generality of souls do not accept the nonsense they hear about judicious indulgence of wrongful inclinations, the influence of non-Christian psychology and pathology is such that many find themselves making concessions to sin which would have been unthinkable had they never come across certain scientific explanations as to how the human mind works. The opinion that, in some people, the results of morally bad inclinations are inevitable, and that therefore to express them is in itself an indifferent or even a good act, is to cut at the roots of free will. No sin is inescapable. No single evil need ever become a necessary, an essential, part of a man's character. To limit moral freedom to certain acts is to deny the doctrine of grace. Once allow the unavoidable circumstance, the paramount claim of physical over spiritual health, the absolute compulsion of heredity or temperament, and you do away with the need to resist temptation. Penance and pardon and reward and merit become meaningless. You might as well give up altogether. Which is what the people who accept these doctrines mostly do. And small wonder: their doctrines give them nothing else to live for.

There are modern writers who hold that though the moral law has a binding force,[*] and that while

---

[*] They give us that.

the individual is expected to train his character in uprightness generally, the sins which a man commits at certain stages of his life or under unusual circumstances are in no way prejudicial either to his ultimate destiny or to his ordinary normal moral life. Thus it is held, for instance, that when a boy is at school, wrestling with the labours of adolescence, or when a man is serving abroad, away from his family, or when he is at sea for a considerable period, or when he is a prisoner — whenever, in effect, he is living outside what might reasonably be called his environment — his lapses are neither reprehensible nor damaging to his character. This is one of the most dangerous fallacies that have ever been invented to shield the wounded conscience of man.

Such conclusions amount to this, that some of man's moral decisions can be here-and-now acts which have no reference to his general direction. It means that sin is something one merely suffers when the mood is on, but which leaves no trace when the occasion is over. It means that one's sin-life operates in a quite different part of one's being from one's ordinary life. "I cannot feel that it is my real self which is sinning. I find that if I let it sweep over me like a storm, I can throw it off and not let it make the slightest difference to everyday existence. So I find that the best thing is to accept the thing more or less passively. And after all, compared with the rest of one's experience, it occupies only a very small sector." This sort of thing is wrong on every possible showing. Even though a man may despise himself for his infidelities, may be disgusted by the sight of so much that is earthy in his composition, may wish he were made of nobler material, if he surrenders to the temptation without a struggle when it presents itself — treating it as the kind of inconvenience which must be expected of an imperfect world — he is a fool to deny his guilt. Though all would agree with Ovid's admission *video meliora proboque, deteriora sequor*, none is thereby excused from blame. How can we say that at any one period of our lives, whether we happen to be at school or at the university or in the army or anywhere else, we are living in a slice of life which does not count? How can we claim that our real lives ended for a time on such and such a date, and began again when the particular interlude was over? No periods, however small, or lived under the pressure of whatever emergency, may be cut from the pattern of our lives. There can be no gap which is made good by merely sewing the ends together: the *post peccatum* going straight on from where the *ante peccatum* left off — and no questions asked.

Sin, then, isn't a separate existence, an unrelated experience. It is a responsible act on every occasion and under whatever conditions. *God* can sort out the question of extenuating circumstances; we can't. Anything which we ourselves do in the way of exculpating is bound to be wrong. At once we become the victims of self-deception, self-commiseration, self-excuse.

Turning to the second error in people's approach to the matter of sin, and one which is quite as common as the first but which can be disposed of much more shortly because the case against it is crystal clear, we come to deal with the person who says: "I know all about God's mercy, but I'm not going to ask for it. He can't want me back after the way I've behaved, and even if I were so underhand as to keep Him to His word and extract a pardon from Him, I should always feel uncomfortable about it. I hate presuming upon anyone's generosity — especially God's." The consequence of this attitude is the same as the consequence of the other: why go on trying? While admitting that there is no such thing as necessary failure (and in this respect differing from the former category) the sinner is faced with the fact that he fails every time the occasion presents itself. He concludes that God must have got tired of expecting his reform, that the doors cannot be left open for ever. "Let me go my own way, and God can wash His hands of me altogether." The faint sniff of humility which, though entirely spurious, is lent to this way of thinking is highly misleading. One feels, in the presence of such an attitude, that the admission is so downright and at the same time so abject that even if it excludes the request for pardon at least it must touch the heart of God. For two reasons this is nonsense: in the first place the disposition is not one of humility, but on the contrary one of obstinacy and despair, and in the second place the heart of God is ready to be touched at any time. What the soul needs to know before all else is that God loves it.

Though we are perpetually being reminded that God loves us, we have the greatest difficulty, when the time comes to benefit by it, in acting upon the knowledge. This means that when we say "God loves me" we are thinking of something which has no relation to what we feel when we love people. It means that in this matter of forgiving, we have never put ourselves in God's place. We have neither projected our own emotions nor given God the credit for behaving as we wouldn't dream of *not* behaving. Can we, for example, imagine ourselves refusing to take back someone whom we are fond of? The person may have neglected us, may have shown repeated weakness and even cruelty, may be addicted to all the ordinary vices, may be unreliable, disloyal, and in fact impossible in every conceivable way, but the moment there is the slightest sign of a return to us the whole weary list of sins is as if it had never been. Long before we are asked to forget the failures of the past we find ourselves hoping against hope that the suggestion will be made. If we love, there is nothing that can stand in the way: forgiveness is such a necessary part of the process that it can be taken for granted. Love *without* the willingness to forgive is no true love. Love is not always able to make us trust the other person, not always able to make us *understand* the other person, but as far as forgiving goes, love is ready with its pardon every day and all day.

Thus if divine love means anything, it means that in what is common to God and ourselves there is not likely to be less generosity on His side than on ours. Human love cannot be better at being merciful than divine. "Nevertheless I am beyond conversion. I have turned over too many new leaves to see the value of doing it again. Each time it has been a failure. I can't go cringing to God at this stage, and be overwhelmed with a forgiveness which I won't be able to keep up. There comes a time when even prodigal sons, after repeated goings and comings, must stay away." But this is where you are so wrong. *Go* cringing to God. It doesn't matter how you go, so long as you go. (In actual fact He prefers you on all fours: if you were to go to Him self-sufficient and thrusting, you would look far more ridiculous.)

With all our faults, with all our worthless past and probable future lapses, with our black record of ingratitude and our somewhat hazy hope of self-reform, we are infinitely more pleasing to God at His feet than at a distance with our backs turned. "Forgive us . . . as we forgive them that sin against us" — and He does.

# SECURITY:
# THE DEMAND FOR IT

WHEN MR. STUART B. JACKman says in his harrowing book *Portrait in Two Colours*, that "nobody really understands life; it's too big, for one thing, and there's too much of it," he is only telling us what our nurses insisted upon when we were small: "You mustn't try and have everything at once; wait till you're older." What we wanted in the nursery was to have all our favourite books read to us at once, all our favourite relations to tea on the same day, all our favourite gramophone records playing while we were having our bath, all our favourite dishes at the same meal, and everything going on at the same time *all the time*. "Wait till you're older," they said. Then we got older, and the great thing we learned about life was that it was too big for us ... and that we would never be able to learn much more than what we knew in the nursery. But the hunger to learn went on; the desire to enjoy everything at once went on. In fact these two appetites, doomed to imperfect realisation in this world, are signs of life. If there were no yearning for comprehension there would be nothing to live for. Even human curiosity can act as a sort of thermometer: the temperature of desire can be too high or too low.

We very soon recognise, in our ideas about happiness, the place of security. That is why, the moment we feel that our happiness is not as secure as it might be, we go out and gather armfuls of straw in the hopes of being able to fill in the threatening cracks and gaps. We are so afraid of being parted from our happiness that we make ourselves miserable insuring ourselves against such a calamity. This side of things does not appear in the nursery: it is only later that we find human nature wanting not only to have experience of every happiness but to hold on to the experience for ever. The insecurity which shoots through every human happiness should convince us that the safest course would be to relax the grip and let it rest in the hollow of our hand for just as long as God wants it there. But experience of happiness does not as a rule teach us this; instead we go on clutching tighter and tighter — and so squeeze out all the essence of it. Sometimes we are so wedded to the *idea* of happiness, to the particular concept of it which we have formed as being suitable to us, that when the chance of real happiness comes along we miss it. We are wedded, and the emphasis is on the less important clause: "to have and to hold" is meaning more to us than the subsequent provision "till God do us part."

The trouble is that almost our only standard of reference with regard to happiness is the past. And the past plays us false. We look back and say: "I was happy then: there was this occasion, and that. I was at such a place, and enjoyed it." We are deluded by the sequence which we see in the past into thinking of happiness in terms of perfect moments. We remember the moments and judge whole years by them, but both happiness and unhappiness need to be seen spread out. Our faces are so close to the pavement of the present, however, that it is not easy to see life spread out. Moments affect life, but they do not constitute it: a series may amount to a state, but it does not constitute one. Happiness and unhappiness are states, not a line of intermittent incidents. Yet, with this faulty perspective of the past in our minds, we run from incident to incident, from refuge to refuge, desperately trying to find our solution, to chain up our experience.

Psychologists tell us, and rightly, that all our obsessions are due either to greed or to fear: desire for more security than we have got, or anxiety lest the security which we possess will be taken away from us. We want to be able to maintain a control which will be absolute—whether over a person or a position or an emotion. In an earlier part of this book it has been suggested, in connection with the question of ambitions, that our hopes are liable to undergo various changes as life moves on. We still want to learn and to have—indeed we want more than ever to learn and to have—but our craving seems to alter its focus. It is not the accumulation urge of the nursery any more, but rather a hunger for certain sureties. Not so much a question now of quantity, but rather one of quality.

One or two solutions is all we want; the toys can be put away. We want to be sure, absolutely sure, that we stand right with regard to God; we want to have the kind of religious certainty which puts us beyond all possible doubt for ever; we want to be sure of those we love—sure of their sanctification, sure of being able to retain their affection, sure that our dealings with them are *right*. In other words we want to leave as little room as possible for the act of faith. With respect to religion it is "I want to *see*"; with respect to people, "I want to *know*." It is not so much that we mistrust either God or those we care for, it is rather that we mistrust ourselves. We never feel quite safe about our own dispositions, our own possible reactions, our own capacity for keeping the thing up. We dread the day when there may *not* be the grace to make the act of faith about religion, and when our feelings are pointing all the other way. What then? We dread the day when the people whose loyalty we can count on now will see through us, and when we shall no longer be able to hold them. What then? We long to be beyond all this: we don't want to have any dreads, either about our beliefs falling to the ground or about our friends going off without us. We want security. We don't like having to trust.

# SECURITY: THE MISTAKE ABOUT IT

WE HAVE SEEN THAT OUR fault lies in wanting to know too much. The tendency goes back to the Garden of Eden. Failure to understand everything, experience everything, manage everything, makes us restless, envious and anxious; we can never feel perfectly at home. But then if we approach life as if it was a fun-fair, we can hardly expect to feel perfectly at home. The reason why we cannot settle down in a fun-fair is because there is far too much fun: there is always another booth just behind us, or a cocoa-nut shy where we're not shying. Also the lights will be turned out before long, and the voice of the merry-go-round will be still. There is only one answer to this hankering for what exceeds our capacity, and that is to be found in the Gospel paradox of losing one's life if one wants to find it. The only security which we shall find on this side of the grave is the security of taking insecurity for granted.

Much has been said in these pages about the necessity of being true to one's particular nature and falling in with the design as it exists in the mind of God. It is in such an idea of conformity (or, considered more personally and as a virtue, of integrity) that the problem of man's restlessness is best met. Many of our unpleasant qualities, as well as many of our miseries, can be put down to the want of truth within ourselves. Often we are difficult to get on with, misfits in our particular society, rebels and at variance with the existing order, not because we are being ourselves but because we are not being ourselves. We are found to be unagreeable, and we on our part find life to be unagreeable, largely because whether we know it or not we are being insincere.

Take an example. People will be pompous, showing the kind of self-importance which Dr. Johnson calls grand nonsense, not because they are too proud to be natural but because they are, very often, too humble to be natural. They feel that they have nothing in the world but their dignity, and so they stand on that. It immediately makes them look ridiculous. The really gifted people do not need to be dignified; they have so much else. Their dignity is unassumed; it is an over-and-above gift which has come without their knowing it; there is no pomposity here. Children are never pompous because they are not conscious of missing anything in their make-up; they do not have to attract people's attention to what is certainly theirs in the hopes that what is wanting to them will not be noticed; everything is theirs. It is only when one gets older, and the gifts of nature begin to wear thin or drop off altogether, that one demands recognition of what is left. The elderly have their dignity; it is their natural right. If they let the young make fools of them, it is for them the end. Thus since nothing invites the ridicule of the younger generation so effectively as the pomposity of the older, we have here a confirmation both of our theory with regard to truth and of the Gospel exhortation with regard to losing one's life and so saving it. In soliciting admiration a man exposes his poverty; in being true to himself, however impoverished, he deserves to be admired. The whole fault lies in pretending, the whole secret in being sincere.

Shyness, again, is due to the same sense of personal insecurity. We are afraid of giving ourselves away. The effort to cling to our self-respect ties us up in knots. The combined effect of dreading to make a bad impression and straining every nerve to make a good one has a petrifying influence on whatever genuine qualities we possess. It is human nature to want, in moments of social stress no less than in more serious situations, to hide behind something or other. When we are embarrassed the screen is sometimes silence, sometimes self-confidence. The mistake is to hide at all. Once we act on the assumption that we are going to make fools of ourselves anyway, we find ourselves no longer self-conscious, inhibited, afraid; nor is there now any need to be thrusting or boastful; we are quite beyond caring. Suddenly we find that we are free to be ourselves. We have let go of what we wanted so eagerly, and behold it has fallen into our hand. All this is in the Gospel if we would only look.

# SECURITY: ITS FOUNDATION

THE ONLY SECURITY TO BE found in this life is that which comes of faith. When this has been said, there doesn't seem much point in saying more. It may be helpful, however, to consider briefly how faith works, and what sort of security it brings. Thus we may know all about the text-book distinctions between historical faith, mathematical faith, theological faith and so on, but unless we know about practical faith—the kind of supernatural certainty which the grace of faith creates in us—we are apt to be disappointed in the results. (The same is the case with the other theological virtues, hope and love: we should not expect them to feel like human hope and human love only more so.) The act of faith does not (any more than does the act of hope or love) depend upon the feelings. This is our great mistake—we think it must. The really important thing to remember is that our safety lies in God and not in our feeling safe.

We may go further and say that true security does not lie in the satisfaction of feeling that the act of faith has gone home and that we can now sit back in the security of our convictions. Faith may or may not produce this sense of safety—and there is every reason to hope that it will—but the essential purpose of faith is to elicit the act of worship which "believes without doubting what God has revealed" and not, primarily, to bring us the consolations of religion. We trust God, we satisfy the conditions, we leave the rest to Him. If, over and above the gift of faith, God grants us the grace of being able to believe in comfort—so much the better. But it is possible to possess the theological virtue of faith without such feelings. The essence of faith is trusting, leaving it to Him, even if we can't be absolutely sure that we *are* trusting and leaving it to Him. "Why hast Thou forsaken me?" we cry with our Lord: we cannot feel that He is anywhere near, but we go on with our act of faith nevertheless. *Forsaken*: what could be stronger than that? Thus we may feel abandoned, but if we cling on in the will—if we *want* to cling on—we are safe. This is real security. There is no lasting security to be found in anything else. Our peace is in God alone. Not in our thoughts about God but in God. If we could put our thoughts about God under a microscope, and discover by analysis that our acts of faith were in perfect working order and that our convictions were on exactly the same level of certainty as the two-and-two-makes-four kind, we would no longer be believing, *we would be seeing*. But blessed are they that have not seen, yet have believed.

The above preamble has been necessary in order to show that what is perhaps our first source of security—or at all events what is instinctively taken to be its defence—may let us down. Namely ourselves. We cannot trust ourselves; we don't know what we shall be feeling next about the things which matter most. We can rely upon God but upon nothing else. God cannot rely upon us, and nor can we. "The man whose heart is set on the law of the Lord," says the psalmist, "stands firm." There lies the answer, setting the heart under the direction of the will. Without the Lord there can be no standing secure. Our own mental, emotional, even spiritual, stability is not to be counted upon: we shall let ourselves down. "What need of aught but thee, Lord, to bring me confidence?" asks the psalmist again. King David knew, if anyone did, the extent of man's unreliability. Fluctuating, swayed by mood, at the mercy of human passion one minute and intellectual prejudice and laziness another, man has precious few resources within himself if he is to find any sort of permanency in this life without God.

If we can't trust ourselves, we certainly can't trust other people. We can't be *sure* of getting lasting happiness from others. "Put not your trust in princes" — and he might have added "or friends." Surely most of us can say, and without either bitterness or self-pity, that there have been occasions when our greatest friends have failed us badly. It may have been our fault, and the thing may have been put right afterwards, but the fact remains that in the experience of our closest relationships there have been times when mutual understanding has broken down. It is the tragedy of so many relationships that such breakdowns are allowed to be complete and utter—when with care, and on the understanding that perfect satisfaction can't be looked for in human creatures, they could be put right. Though this may sound disillusioned, it is surely not merely the wisdom of the world which suggests that temporary betrayals are to be expected between people who are fond of one another. Deplored but expected. Human nature is unstable; people *are* disloyal. Yes, even when they love each other, men and women are hopelessly unpredictable. Perhaps all the more *because* they are in that strange state. Listen to Maurice Baring: "'Being in love' is only a label in shorthand; the real contents of the thing is loving, suspecting, not loving, believing, becoming indifferent, minding awfully, *von Hertzen, mit Schmertzen, klein und wenig, garnicht—über alle Massen.*" No, you can't find what you want there. But though human love may fall far short of providing the solution which you are looking for, it provides something instead which is far better for you. It provides you the occasion of making the act of faith—both in the person, and, more conclusively, in God. Trust is security, and security is trust; that's all ye know, and all ye need to know.

# SECURITY: ITS OPERATION

YOU WILL SAY THAT SECURITY cannot *operate*. The whole point about security is, you will say, that it is stable—static and not dynamic. So it would seem perhaps, yet on the other hand if we accept the findings of the last two or three essays we see that there is plenty of scope in our idea of security for the element of change. Serenity, if we follow out the argument, comes as much from assimilating change as from enjoying order and balance. In fact rather more. We have suggested that the human mind can rest at peace only when it has reached the conclusion that there can be no such thing, humanly speaking, as resting at peace. The assurance of security lies in the conviction of faith and not in the experience of tranquillity. "Man's life and the life around him," says Walter de la Mare, "are but the flotsam of perpetual flux."* Surely the truth is that the substance is stable and that the accidents vary. *Plus ça change, plus c'est la même chose*. Once we have got this right, we stand at least some chance of resting secure.

---

\* This is perhaps going a bit far, but then the writer is merely throwing off the observation in a short story (*All Hallows*), and not giving his views as a serious philosopher. Mr. de la Mare does not as a rule regard man as being flotsam.

In one of Tchekov's more depressing stories, *My Life*, the author says that if he were to put an inscription inside his ring, he would alter King David's "Everything passes" (which is echoed in the last act of Noel Coward's *Cavalcade*) to "Nothing passes." This is all very challenging. The answer is that both statements are true, and that in either case there is room for cynicism and congratulation at the same time. You can look at it one way, and say that because life goes on without you it is no use trying to cling to the day-to-day experience of it. Or you can look at it the other way, and think of it as experience staying behind after all the contributing causes, the moments, have passed. Indeed it is necessary, if we are to avoid disappointment, to look at life from both these points of view; they are not contradictory, they are complementary. The first warns us against living in the past and being over-possessive about the present, the second tells us that we cannot shake off what we have learned of life and go on as if it had never had any effect. Many of our trials would be spared us if these two principles were better understood.

"Everything passes": our failures pass as readily, thank God, as surely as do our successes. The words should inspire more hope than they do reflex wistfulness. It is not in the nature of man to be miserable for ever, and given a cloud he will instinctively look for the lining of silver... given a corner he will expect, in spite of himself, a joy to come round it. "I know all about that," you will say, "but before there's been time to think, along comes another cloud and another corner. Nothing can ever be pinned down." Quite so; but on the other hand it is of the essence of human enjoyment that pleasure should be transitory. What if we *could* halt the passage of time? Would not all the other contributing causes of our happiness fall rather flat? In this life we have not the equipment which would enable us to *possess* happiness: it would wear thin or become cloying if we had too much of it. We have been provided with the apparatus necessary for the enjoyment of human happiness, and in each of the terms of reference the transitory element is an essential one. In heaven we shall be provided with all the apparatus necessary for the enjoyment of supernatural happiness. And that will be a very different matter.

"Nothing passes": the natures we are born with, our manners, habits, tendencies, prejudices, eccentricities . . . all these remain horribly the same throughout our lives. Yes, but there is much more in it than this. It means that not only what we start off with accompanies us all the way, but also what each of our decisions has *built up on what we have started off with* accompanies us all the way. And *that* is why we can never say of any sin "it doesn't mean anything, it isn't really an indication of me at all." *That* is why every effort, however small, is immeasurably valuable on the positive side. All our lives we are either constructing or destroying, and each constructive act is not only, judged singly, one to the good; it is a contribution which makes the next contribution more possible, more easy to elicit. Nothing passes — without making the way clear for something of the same kind to pass again. If a weak person does a strong thing, he is more likely to do another strong thing than if he had stuck to the practice of doing weak ones. However weak a person is, or however strong a person is, the repetition of the act must, for good or for evil, transform the person's character.

Thus whichever way you take it, there is this much comfort to be got from the "Everything passes" of King David[*] and the "Nothing passes" of Tchekov, that though opportunities may have been wasted, there is still the supreme opportunity of profiting by your experience — even if you have experienced nothing but waste. Experience is the most costly thing in the world, so it might as well be made use of. It is certainly the best approach to the present opportunity. Having paid the price of failure, temptation, mistake, suffering and regret, man should have something more to show for his experience than sterile memories; at least let him have the knowledge of what he may do with the immediate now. Experience is like a river which bit by bit widens the course of its flowing. By every ripple that comes along, the banks are being gradually nibbled away. Life goes by and we can't do anything to stop it; all the time we are recovering some sort of impression, suffering some sort of alteration. The stream passes,

---

[*] Not forgetting Mr. Coward.

but not without its legacy: life passes, but not without its widened opportunity.

Moreover, whatever else is seen to be transitory, the existence of grace is a constant. Graces may have been wasted, but the stream of grace has not dried up. "All these things shall pass away, but my word shall not pass away." Though the natural may provide unpromising material, there is still the supernatural to be considered. Our security lies in the supernatural and not in the natural.* The supernatural may not bring us quite the kind of security which most of us want, but this is not the supernatural's fault—it is ours. "The just man liveth by faith." The trouble is that we are not sufficiently just; if we were, we should find less difficulty in living by faith. (The proposition works with equal truth the other way round: if we were more ready to live by faith, there would be no problem about being just.)

---

\* *The One remains, the many change and pass;*
*Heaven's light for ever shines, earth's shadows fly;*
*Life, like a dome of many-coloured glass,*
*Stains the white radiance of eternity. . . .*
                                     Shelley, *Adonais*.

# PERSEVERANCE IN FAITH

IF WE WANT TO KNOW ABOUT faith we cannot do better than study the eleventh chapter of the Epistle to the Hebrews. Faith, the author tells us in the first verse, gives us sure and absolute conviction of things which without faith we would never be able to see. It is God's gift. It is necessary for us in the work which He has given us to do, and therefore we can count on being given enough of it: God, in proposing a supernatural purpose to man, pledges Himself to supernatural assistance. The soul of man is designed to find its ultimate rest in God. While still on this earth, man is called upon to worship God by faith, and this he does by making use of the gift. The gift, this necessary gift, is there. Yet man, with his accompanying and frightening gift of free will, can deny it. In fact, man can do what he likes with it: he can accept it, extend it, limit it, live by it, pretend that he has himself fashioned it, go back on it, and eventually stifle it. The only thing he cannot do is to claim, while possessing it, that he owes no obligations towards it.

Faith convinces us of the reality not only of the things which we cannot see but also of those which we cannot feel. And this touches most of us more closely.

The existence of the Blessed Trinity puts hardly any strain upon our faith: we have never seen the Blessed Trinity but we accept the doctrine with alacrity. As a rule it is not the articles of the Creed which test our faith; the test comes when we have to override our feelings. The gift of faith may certainly be exposed to danger if we either begin to question its tenets or neglect its safeguards, but there is no danger so menacing as that to which it is open when we decide to put our faith in our feelings. Faith and morals go together, and in an age when morals are to a large extent guided by mood it is inevitable that mood should similarly try and dominate belief. We shall have more to say about the cinema morality and the cotton-wooled conscience of the present day; here we can confine ourselves to the question of faith.

When it seems to us that our prayers are nothing but a "vain repetition," an empty superstition, a survival of a childhood resolution, a complete and somewhat hypocritical waste of time, *then* do we have to draw upon the gift of faith, When God appears to have lost interest in our affairs, when His demands seem hopelessly impersonal and unrelated to existing conditions, when the whole of His dealings with man is felt as the imposition of a system and not as the creation of a bond, then is faith particularly necessary to us. In those moods of mental weariness when we find ourselves wondering whether material things may not have a purely material origin and purpose after all, whether all human trials may not have their own human explanation, whether every problem and difficulty may not admit of a straightforward daylight solution if only we were alert enough or clever enough (or scientifically advanced enough or psychologically adjusted enough) to recognise and understand the answer, then comes faith to "let us understand how the world was fashioned by God's word; how it was from the things unseen that the things we see took their origin." Sight and feeling on one side, clamouring for recognition; faith on the other, ready to give the last word. Sight and feelings, up in arms and talking about proof... faith doing duty for both of them.

Sometimes the intellect lets us down, sometimes the heart: sometimes both together. "I'm very much afraid He doesn't really exist, le bon Dieu," complains the sculptor, Durien, in *Trilby*, and he adds at once— "most unfortunately for me, for I *adore* Him." There are periods when adoration (if it is a shade more effective than Durien's) rescues from doubt, and there are other periods when reason can be relied upon to support a flagging love. But all the time faith has to be there to feed the will.

"Nobody reaches God's presence until he has learned to believe that God exists," the same Epistle to the Hebrews informs us. Yes, we say, but how do we go on from there? In the rest of the verse we are told the answer: we believe that "God rewards those who try to find Him." *Try to*. The whole point is here; this is where the will to accept God's gift comes in. There is no mention, yet, of success. Thirty-three verses lower down we are told that the great examples of faith — Noe, Abraham, Isaac, Moses, Gideon and the rest were men who "never saw the promise fulfilled." This was their merit, this was their success, this was why they were held up to us to follow — *that they went on looking.*

# PERSEVERANCE IN WORK

IF FAITH IN GOD IS EXPRESSED by persevering in belief under the attack of doubt, faith in the work which God has given us to do is expressed in perseverance under the attack of opposition, weariness, restlessness and impulse. Just as to know all about perseverance in faith we have to know the agonies of mistrust and the cold bleak approaches to unbelief, so in order to know all about perseverance in work we have to have a pretty good idea of laziness and the sweets of leisure. In other words, if we know the work to be from God, we go on with it. Faith and labour: we worship God with both: that is primarily what they are for.

Belief, whether in God or in a cause or in a person, can be proved only by constancy. Constancy depends on the set of the will, and so takes no more account of the feelings than it does of the weather. The sense of incapacity, the risings of anxiety, disgust and so on are swept aside by the man who is constant, by the man who has faith. He expects these distracting emotions to arise — they are, though accidental, inescapables — but he laughs at them. He *believes*. Belief in this sense, which is three parts hope and one part muleheaded obstinacy, refuses to bow to statistics, disappointment, argument — or indeed to anything except the signified will of God. Such a belief has about it that same hard bright flamelike quality in its idealism which makes for independence as well as endurance. It gives courage where there was none before. Out of nonentities it can make heroes. In politics, for example, it can produce a leader; in art, an originator; in the social order, a reformer. Harnessed to an unworthy cause this fixity of belief and purpose can do untold harm; found in an unstable subject it can produce mania. On the debit side the danger is fanaticism, on the credit side the reward is sanctity. The tests are always perfectly clear: obedience, consistency, and perseverance.

The beauty of this kind of heroism lies in the fact that it need not be spectacularly heroic. Therefore it is open to all. In fact, the less there is of outward display the better. No organ plays, no trumpet blows, when we simply go on with our work. Having fixed principles and abiding by them, or even having one lodestar idea and following it to the ends of the earth, need not involve publicity. Here is a case in point.

A certain young priest showed promise as a lecturer in philosophy and theology. After a year or two of this work he was sent, by the superiors of the religious congregation to which he belonged, to the Indian mission. Here he spent the next twenty-three years of his life, and was then retired to the novitiate house in England. Soon afterwards, however, the Indian mission finding itself in need of men, the now ageing priest was asked to go back. He was told he could take up exactly the same work where he had left off, and that he could expect every assistance from home, every blessing of God upon his labours, every welcome from his native flock in India. Shortly before he left England, a friend came to see him to say goodbye. The following conversation took place. The friend: "You must be glad that you're not on the shelf. You will feel more at home in the work you've been used to abroad." The missioner: "Possibly. But, you know, I've hated that work all along." The friend: "Those twenty-three years? You mean you didn't like them?" The missioner: "They were hell." The friend: "But why didn't you get yourself brought home sooner?" The missioner: "It might not have been the thing." (Pause.) The friend: "Anyway, as you are still here, the obvious plan is to stay. You could easily be put on as a lecturer in the house of studies: you liked that, and were good at it. It seems absurd to go back to India and to the life that doesn't suit you." The missioner: "I suppose one ought to leave these things to God, oughtn't one?" Back he went to India where he is now.

The names cited in the eleventh chapter of Hebrews are a roll of honour to those who have persevered. The list commemorates those who have been true to their nature as Hebrew idealists and who have kept up the struggle till their last breath. They never for a moment lost faith in their mission. It was their work, it was their worship, it was their means to sanctity. Their names were chosen because names have to be chosen if conspicuous examples are to be given of a virtue. For them, certainly, there has been the red carpet and the roll of drums. But perseverance is just as possible without. (While even in the case of the patriarchs the recognition was mostly posthumous.) What does the virtue essentially consist in? In nothing more than plain surrender to the designs of God; no pulling of strings or forcing the convenient solution, no listening to excuses, no turning away from obedience or dullness or conscience — *and then not stopping for anybody or anything.*

If anyone[*] tells you that by going on working when you are exhausted, or ill, or not in the mood, you are only doing yourself harm and producing no good work, do not believe him. You are, on the contrary, doing yourself a great deal of good and at the same time producing the best possible kind of work. If it is God's work that you are supposed to be doing, the more you do of it the better. The effort is the goodness of the work. If the effort is shown at its best when all the pull is in the opposite direction, then let exhaustion, mood, health, age and the rest of them do their worst: nothing can spoil the work. "God asketh not a perfect work," says St. Catherine, "but infinite desire." It is one

---

[*] That is anyone who has no authority over you. Clearly obedience alters the whole situation. Thus it may be a duty to stop one form of work when exhausted or ill in order to attend to another which is more directly connected with obedience.

of the world's foremost misconceptions that it takes the perfect outward achievement as the sole criterion of worth. The desire, and if possible the work as well, must go on to the end. The one helps out the other, they are cause and effect.

To believe in one's work means to live in it. And, if this can be managed, to die at it. Velasquez who painted till he could no longer see the colours on the canvas, Monet who went on till he could no longer hold a brush, Irving and Sarah Bernhardt and Duse who acted till they dropped, Hallé who conducted till he couldn't lift either arm to wave a baton, Blake who died composing (and singing) verse ... these are men and women who believed in their work. One might alter Disraeli's statement already referred to, and say that if you want to know what perseverance is like you can go and live among artists. Other callings could of course produce their parallel columns of names; the above are simply the cases which immediately spring to the mind. But whatever the calling in which our particular interest lies, we would-be followers of Christ are often put to shame by the sight of such fidelity and purpose, since for us (to quote for the last time from the Epistle to the Hebrews) "God has something better in store" — than the reward of an art or of a profession faithfully served.

# PERSEVERANCE
# IN PRAYER

APPLY THE GIST OF THE foregoing chapters to the subject of prayer, and you see where it leads us. We go on praying not merely in the hope of being answered, but in the conviction of being heard. Prayer, that is to say, is an expression of worship before it is a means of obtaining things. As an expression of worship, prayer can never fail; as a means of obtaining things its success is qualified by the kind of things it obtains—or, more strictly, by the way in which the return is made. Considered simply as worship, the act of prayer is the most direct that man can make. It is more worth while than any other. "What about charity?" If you had an act of prayer-charity and an act of neighbour-charity alongside one another, and if they both measured the same degree of respective love, the prayer act would—if they were not the same thing and *could* be compared with each other—rank higher. Charity is love, is prayer. Works of charity are, like any other works, expressions of worship. Love is worship itself. That is why we have said that prayer is the most direct act of worship which man can make. Where other acts may worship by means of neighbour, by means of ceremonial, by means of words or works, the act of love (which is what we mean by the prayer act at its highest and in its most complete form) quite simply worships.

Still considering: the prayer of praise, and not yet the prayer of petition, it is clear that there can be no other gauge or standard with which to assess it than that of its continuance: do you go on with it or do you give it up? Certainly the degree of worship must vary with the generosity of the soul who prays — and there are a number of other factors which may come in, affecting the balance favourably or adversely — but so far as applying a test to the prayer itself goes, the rule is as absolute as it is obvious. Are you or are you not prepared to persevere in prayer?

Again and again in the Gospel our Lord tells us to go on repeating our prayer; the saints, by their own example as well as by their preaching, insist upon the same thing; we get it in the catechism, in the liturgy, in the encyclicals, in the Fathers and spiritual writers. The language of love is the language of repetition . . . the habit of worship cannot be launched and kept up on a single act . . . perseverance is the sole guarantee of good faith. We learn all this from others, and even in our own experience the knowledge is confirmed by the story of our failure and success. If correspondence, unremitting and sometimes very much against a protesting self, is found to be necessary in human relationships, it is no less necessary in maintaining a relationship which is divine. The whole matter is as clear as the cloudless sky. Nevertheless "my prayers can't possibly be doing any good . . . people seem to manage without praying, so why shouldn't I? . . . I never seem to get what I want . . . it feels so absurd . . . what is the use of saying the same words over and over again when you can't pay any attention to them? . . . what is the use of mooning about in the belief that you're practising mental prayer? . . . what is the use of wasting time which would be better employed doing almost anything else but this endless business of pretending to pray." This is simply nature objecting to the duty of worship which it is beginning to find boring. Nature must not be listened to: of course it finds the work boring. How could it be anything else — day after day and no concrete result which you can point to and say "That's what my labour has brought me." The fact that it is only faith which can say that the labour has been worth while provides yet one more stumbling block to nature. If it had been feelings, now, instead of faith which let one know the value of one's effort, it would be so much easier to go on . . . but to have to do it all on faith . . . when obviously it isn't doing one any good. Always we get back to the plaintive echo: "What's the use?"

"I could understand it being dull and apparently fruitless if the whole business of prayer were simply praise and nothing else," a soul will say, "but I should have thought that at least in the case of petition, which is about the only kind of prayer which most of us rise to, there would be more to show for it and consequently more interest in actually trying to practise it." In the first place, the prayer of petition is praise — since by asking for what he wants, the petitioner pays homage to the Giver of gifts — and so is governed by the same conditions. If it is in the nature of praise to require persistency in the exercise of faith, willingness to endure boredom, constant restatement of the act, then these things must be part of petition as well. The same is true of thanksgiving and reparation, which, with praise and petition, make up the four main expressions of prayer. "But this doesn't explain" — the soul may go on to object — "why my petitions, even when I have persevered with them, so often remained unanswered. It would surely encourage me to pray more if I knew I would eventually get what I wanted." Some paragraphs, then, on the subject of petitions.

Two people in the same family are praying for mutually exclusive intentions: the brother prays that the household may move to another part of the country, the sister that it may stay where it is. Therefore the first fact about the prayer of petition is that all requests cannot, physically, be granted. As to which of two conflicting intentions is heard, you may say that all things being equal the prayer which is made by the holier soul, or by the soul who prays harder and with greater love, is the one which will be answered. This is why we ask holy people to pray for us: we know that their prayers are likely to carry more weight than our own. "This certainly challenges one's generosity," it might be admitted, "but the clause 'all things being equal' allows for the rejection of even the holiest people's requests." That the brother or sister in the above example who prays harder and longer and in altogether better dispositions may have to see the other's comparatively effortless prayer being answered is undoubtedly possible. It would mean in this case that more important issues were involved than those envisaged by the person praying. It would not mean that the projected move had been hardly worth praying about; on the contrary it would mean that the projected move had been so worth praying about that two people had been urged by the movement of grace to make it their intention.

When God wishes to bring about a certain result, He may either produce the effect directly or else make use of the agencies which He has created. Normally He follows the latter course. Consequently when God wants to confer a certain benefit upon an individual He gives him the grace to pray for it and so, in a sense, to earn it. It is like a rather complicated game — God giving us the money to buy the present to give to Him to elicit the good which He has been going to give us all along. The fact that He has been going to give it to us all along makes no difference to the necessity of praying for it. We go on praying until we get it. Again the absolute need, in this matter of petition, of perseverance: there may be numberless gifts which were designed for us in God's plan but which have not come to us because we have not gone on asking for them. What we have to bear in mind is that by endowing us with the power of effectively praying for things, God has, on His side, a twofold purpose in view: He wants to have us praying to Him; He wants to hear our prayer. So of course He does not hear us at once — or *that* particular petition of ours would cease. Of course He wants us to go on — or according to the rules of the game He must keep back what He is waiting to give us.

"This seems to tie God's hands," will be the comment at the present stage in the argument; "because if God is kept waiting with the gifts which He wants to give us, His freedom is made dependent upon the activity of man." No more than God's mercy is made dependent upon man's decision to ask for it. And no less. The two are on a par. God tells us what to do to obtain His favours, and then leaves it to us to decide. By neglecting to take the means which are provided for us at every turn, we tie our own hands, not His.

A final objection may take another form, and one which is as understandable as any. "Leaving aside such cases as conflicting need, and assuming that we have prayed hard and long for a certain unquestionably good intention, it is disheartening to conclude either that God isn't satisfied with the most generous effort of which we are capable or else that we have a mistaken idea about what is unquestionably good." Say we pray for a person's conversion and it does not come about, for a person's recovery from an illness and he gets worse, for a person's happy marriage and his wife leaves him after six months. The results have turned out to be disappointing, but the prayers have not been *rejected*. No prayer is wasted, no prayer fails to register. Every prayer, however flatly contradicted by subsequent events, is one act of worship to the good. Not only as regards God are such prayers acts of praise, and as regards us occasions of merit, but even as regards the people we have been praying for they were channels of grace. So in that sense they are not unheard prayers at all. The fact that the graces — which our prayers have been instrumental in procuring — were in the event rejected does not alter the efficacy of the prayer. The sinner in question has had a grace offered to him but he has not taken it, the sick man has been given something which he needed more than health, the husband has been strengthened to meet the disillusionment about his wife.

To conclude. God moves us to ask for things. These things either come to us or they do not. If they do, then it means that we have both recognised the terms of His inspiration and faithfully correspond. If they do not, then either we have not prayed hard enough and long enough or we have misunderstood the nature of the inspiration and our prayer has been heard in another direction. What has happened in this latter case is simply this, that God, seeing into the heart of man far more deeply than man himself can see, and reading there of a need which man himself knows little about, urges the man to pray his way out of the problem. In this way it can very easily happen that souls, mistaking their real need and praying for a certain definite solution which to them seems the reasonable one, are on the look-out for quite the wrong answer to their prayer. To them, with their limited and all too human vision, the thing which they are praying for is seen as unquestionably good, immediately necessary, and alone capable of meeting the need. But then they have never really seen the need; their prayer has reflected only a part of it. God is not now, on the strength of this mistaken conception, going to tie these souls down to the actual terms of their prayer and so deprive them of what He originally meant them to ask for. What does He do? He does what we should do if we were dealing with imperfectly enlightened subjects — He takes their prayer and answers it in His terms and not in theirs. He gives always what is better, God's better inevitably surpasses man's best. Yet man goes on with "What's the use? . . . I never get what I ask for . . . what's the use?"

# PERSEVERANCE IN EVERYTHING

*I*T IS OUR PRINCIPLE THAT LIFE comes from God and that it must be returned to Him as He wants it. It is our policy that we bear out this principle in work, in human intercourse, in the shaping of our thought. On these foundations we take our stand as Christians. Having confidence in a principle and a policy follows the same course as having confidence in God or in a person or in anything else. All it means is holding out against persuasion to the opposite.

We have seen that to believe in God is to refuse to be put off by His absence, and that to believe in a person is to refuse to be put off by his failure. What we now have to see is that to believe in the principle and policy of life, life as we assume it to have been planned for us by God, is to refuse to be put off by anything.

The constancy of the saints can be accounted for only by the quality and the direction of their desires. "The country of their desires," we read in the Epistle to the Hebrews, "is a better, a heavenly country." Desires which rule out all possibility of surrender are not the monopoly of the saints; they can be ours just as much. Such desires feed, and for their part are fed by, faith. Not any power in the world can withstand the combination of faith and desire. It is this combination which perseveres even against the opposition of self.

The greatest obstacle to this trust, to this perseverance, is ourselves. Of the devil, the world, and the flesh (those perennial companions), it is the flesh which has the most say. The devil tempts, but it is we who listen; the world preaches its gospel, but it is we who act on it. The devil and the world between them, by exposing our weakness and pointing to the futility of resisting further, are the disruptive influences; but it is we who bear out their argument by our surrender. We give in, not because the world forces us to or because we know from our experience that we are not cast in the heroic mould, but simply because we give in. The saints are those who do not listen to the flesh, do not listen to themselves. So long as they are ready to "welcome God's promises at a distance," waiting for them to be realised in heaven, it doesn't matter what they feel about them on the spot.

"I buffet my own body," says St. Paul to the Corinthians, "and make it my slave." Any other course is fatal. If we allow ourselves to be guided by what the body says, we have as good as ceased to struggle. It is always the body which says that penance need not be kept up, that prayer is a waste of time, that work as a God-given duty is overrated, that health and peace and comfort and advancement and being in good spirits are more important than anything else. "I do not run my course like a man in doubt of his goal," explained St. Paul — so he could afford to be rough with the feelings of the body. If ours is the same goal, ours must be the same faith — the faith which flogs the last ounce out of our bodies, which spurs the last totter out of our lives.

Here is a story that could serve as an end-paper to any of the four books in the present sequence.

There was a certain uncle who, whenever he was in London and was not dining out early, used to visit his nephew, aged six and a half, and tell him stories at bed-time. The uncle did not much enjoy the custom, and the stories were not outstandingly good ones, but he felt that it was the sort of thing which was expected of an uncle and so he kept it up. The small boy on his side — one has to face these facts — did not much enjoy the custom either; but he too felt that the practice, being eminently suitable to both parties, should be maintained. "Besides, this particular uncle," he reflected one evening when his visitor had left himself less time than usual in which to dress for dinner, "needs encouragement." In the minds of both the uncle and the nephew the nightly routine came to have an almost religious significance — and indeed there were elements such as unselfishness, the need to focus attention, the effort to keep awake, which bore this out — so that it was with a certain sense of guilt that they each looked forward to the eighth birthday which was tacitly taken to mark the end of an epoch.

One evening, whether because the uncle was feeling

more tired than the nephew or whether because the stock of giants, princesses, witches, and dragons had run low, there was a long silence after the end of night prayers ... while each hoped that someone would come in and say it was getting late. "You tell *me* a story for a change," said, surprisingly, the uncle. The small boy, though shocked by this departure from the accepted tradition, took up the challenge. This is the story he told.*

There was once a very brave general who used in person, and much against the advice of his staff, to lead his armies into battle. The soldiers, however, had none of the courage of their leader, and when from time to time during the heat of the conflict the general felt it his duty to leave the front line and seek out some vantage point on the field so as the better to see what was going on, the troops would invariably fall back. This was so noticeable that the less timorous of the officers, as soon as they saw the general sheathing his sword and slipping away into the background with his maps and his field-glasses, used to press their horses forward towards the enemy, dismount, and do a sort of dance before their own wavering lines. Even so it was as much as they could do to keep the battle going at all.

Thus it came about on one occasion that having been the first to take the field and having successfully withstood the impact of the charge, the general, in

---

\* The narrative style of the original has been altered to suit the text; the substance of the story remains unchanged.

accordance with his usual habit, climbed a hill a little way off and began to take stock of the engagement. It was as if a signal had been given to retire: the troops, ignoring the encouragement of their officers, turned their sorry backs upon the advancing enemy. The general, who was now in full view of his men, not only shouted exhortations but sang to them at the top of his voice the most stirring ballads he knew. So great, however, was the din of battle that the brave man's words carried little beyond the raised ground on which he had stationed himself: tactical instructions and noble sentiments were alike wasted: the troops continued to fall back. It was evening, and the red-gold sun was setting behind the figure of the mounted man. Outlined back against the sky the old warrior was a reproach, a symbol, a challenge. But whether because the retreating soldiers could not see the tears of shame and disappointment streaming down his cheeks or because they were too busy running, the spectacle had no meaning for them. Then three things happened. First a cannon-ball struck the general's horse and killed it outright—leaving the general standing now upon his own two feet. Then another cannon-ball came and shot away the general's right leg at the hip. Quick as light the general drew his sword from the scabbard at his left side, and, with a sweep which caught the last rays of sun, dug its tip in the ground beneath him. Leaning upon his sword as if it were a stick, the general, with the arm which was still free, made signs to his men that they were to re-engage the enemy. But before there was time for the men to interpret the order—let alone obey it—a third cannon-ball flew over their heads and took away the other leg. What the army saw now was the silhouette of their leader supported by a sword on one side and a scabbard on the other: it was as if he were on crutches, and his knuckles pressed the grass. This was the last the soldiers saw of their general, for a great roar went up from the whole field, and, as if by one man's word of command, the entire force turned and plunged into the ranks of the oncoming enemy.

That was the end of the story. The uncle never knew, therefore, whether the battle was won or lost. Because, though the nephew thought[*] it was a good story, he didn't seem to think it mattered how it went on beyond the place where he had decided to put the full stop. The uncle was inclined to think that defeat would, artistically, make a better conclusion than victory. Anyway there were no more stories that night; the uncle knew when he was beaten. But from then onwards until the relieving eighth birthday, the stories, whenever the uncle was in London, went on. How, after that particular story, could they not?

---

[*] And still thinks.

# CHILDREN

HAT WE ALL ASK FROM life, though we do not always admit it to ourselves, is that somewhere, somehow, in some capacity, or to someone, we should be indispensable. We want the satisfaction of knowing that our place in the scheme of creation is assured to this extent, that were either our labour, our advice, or our presence to cease its exercise of influence in one or other particular direction, there would be the most awful and obvious gap. Ignoble it may be, but it is one of the characteristics of man that he likes the feeling of being missed. Accordingly when we find that the world can manage just as well without our services as with them, we find at the same time that the field narrows itself down to the strictly personal: what we ask now is that there may be at least one person on earth who will put us before every other created thing and keep us there. More than wanting to rely on other people, we want other people to rely on us. This is the first reason why we like children.

Not only do we hope to come across someone who will take us to be the most important factor, the only important factor, in human life, but we hope also that the person will say it and show it — go on saying it and go on showing it. Bad as this would be for us if it ever happened, we can see how it is that the greatest human joy must be that of a mother. To know that here is a person, even though a very young person, who looks to one for everything, whose leaning upon one is without shame or reflex worries of any sort, whose affection is in no way put off by one's looks or one's age or one's stupidity, who takes it for granted that there will never be any rivals, who brushes aside quarrels like crumbs, must be as satisfactory as anything can be in this world. There can be nothing like it. Thus intelligent mothers need be neither blind nor, as we think, self-deceived in their love for what sometimes appear to be detestable children: they are receiving something which can compensate for all the unpleasant qualities which a child can possibly possess.

It is not only because we long to be believed in, and because we fear that our own generation will see through us, that we like to be with young people. Many of us probably prefer to be with young people rather than with grown-ups because we feel at home with them. When Charles Dodgson was being the don he stuttered; he didn't stutter at all when he was being Lewis Carroll with his little girls. In some people the childhood mould of mind never breaks, and they go on for ever being in their element with the young. The interests, the particular brand of rather rare humour, the unlikely enthusiasms and unreasonable fears have somehow stayed behind while the rest of their nature has matured. This does not for a moment mean that such people are childish or even inexperienced in the ways of the world; it merely means that they have a more unclouded vision, a less *verdinglicht* approach. To them the world of youth is the real world and they return to it whenever they possibly can. The chilling phrase "being good with young people" doesn't mean being able to assume the manner and idiom (heaven forbid); it means that where most of us find pleasure in the company of the young and adolescent either because they are a relief after the sophisticated, or because they are stimulating, or because they laugh at our jokes, or because they remind us of our own early years, the people who are "good with the young" are those who possess the secret of being natural outwardly in a world which is only inwardly theirs.

What experience gives with one hand it takes away with the other, and perhaps what many of us are doing in our youthful contacts is trying to borrow back what life has taken from us. Innocence appears to us not only as a good, but as *our* good. We want to see more of it. We are always hoping to discover the formula which will open the door to it, which will let us move in and taken possession again. We look forward to being led back, in Miss Elizabeth Bowen's phrase, "to that early morning world without brushing the dew off the grass." Even if our friendships do no more than create for us this illusion, we should be grateful to them: there is nothing wrong with an atmosphere, however transient and bitter-sweet, which makes us want the things that are of God. Souls for whom there is never any dew, never any grass, never any sparkle of early morning, must find maturity very soul-destroying. If anyone should say to this that he is a realist, and (throwing out his chest) that he has no use for those who live in a dream world of fantasy, it shows that he has missed the whole point. Such a man has lost one wisdom and not learned another; he has no longer the freedom of familiar things and has not yet attained to a knowledge of the rare. He should know that innocence, ignorance, inexperience, are not the opposites of wisdom and reality, and that sometimes it is both more wise and more honest to try and live once again in the untutored world where the edges of right and wrong have not been filed down by excuses, concessions and precedent. The opposites of wisdom and truth are folly and unreality, and there is far more of both among grown men and women than there is ever likely to be discovered among the young.

So far in this review of motives we have considered the love of children and young people chiefly from the point of view of what the searcher is hoping to get out of them. We have seen that at best he looks to youth as to a magic looking-glass — always for some sort of reflexion of himself. In the search among those much younger than himself, in that yearning for the companionship of children which at times amounts almost to a physical ache, man is reaching out towards something more important than himself. He is looking for God.

> *I turned me to them very wistfully;*
> *But just as their young eyes grew sudden fair*
> *With dawning answers there,*
> *Their angel plucked them from me by the hair.*

If Francis Thompson is here considering less the innocence and loveliness of small children than the emptiness and loneliness of having to do without them it is because of the particular nature of his experience. That children grow up and leave us — mothers can be the unhappiest people in the world as well as the happiest — does not alter the fact that we are looking for God in them before they go. Nor is it surprising that Francis Thompson should see the right thing the wrong way round — since in any case he saw himself fleeing from God when in fact he was groping towards Him.

# SIMPLICITY IN ART

DIVINE ATTRIBUTES ARE BEST approached on the knees. Certainly with regard to beauty we learn more by praying than by doing anything else about it. Natural beauty and supernatural beauty are not two different things, but two different aspects of the same thing. The true artist cannot decide to follow the natural and ignore the supernatural; aesthetics cannot forge ahead without paying any attention to ethics. These are facts which are constantly being denied by artists who have no intention of either cultivating the supernatural or curbing the natural, so it would be as well that we should get the principle perfectly clear. Our claim is, then, that created beauty reveals itself in its perfection only to those who come to it with something more than a visual appreciation. The maximum enjoyment of creatures requires more than the mere minimum recognition of their Creator. If the artist stands by his proposition that he is the complete man, the last thing he can afford to leave out is religion. The man who is more complete still, we would hold, is the saint.

If it is the clean of heart who shall see God, it is the clean of sight who shall see the best that is in God's works. To look for anything else in art but goodness, truth and beauty is to miss what is essentially there to be revealed. Look in it for self, and you cease to see anything else. Ask of it something base, and it withers altogether. You may see something else which you mistake for beauty, but as far as you are concerned beauty is already dead.

Perfection, whether in art or in work or in people, has its own dignity which is designed to protect it against the cupidity of those who pay it tribute. Thus the true artist, glimpsing beauty for the first time, is moved not at once to self-indulgence but to wonder. It is only if his respect wears thin and his gaze is turned back upon himself that he feels the desire to possess. This is his first test: whether to be content to bow in homage or whether to reach out and grab.

The artist ceases to be a true artist the moment be loses the simplicity of his vision. If he interprets beauty in terms which are not true, if he attracts attention to himself and not to the beauty which it is his gift and mission to reveal, if he begins to wallow, he not only fails in his service to God and to his fellow man and to his profession, but he destroys his own powers of perception. He may be able to *observe* things, he may be able to do what he likes with them in whatever medium he chooses, he may find satisfaction in expressing himself through them, he may be hailed as a genius and go down in history as a master, but if he does not keep his eye on what he is meant to see he is no true artist.

If beauty is the sheen of order, then the less there is of multiplicity about both its recognition and its expression the better. Order can exist only where there is harmony of purpose in the various departments which go to make up the whole, and where the faculties or instruments are employed according to their nature. This is true of an institution, of a system, of a person, of a piece of mechanism. Order may be busy and it may be noisy, but it can never be fussy. Painting and politics and prayer and education — indeed enterprise of any sort, even propaganda and publicity — can all express themselves loudly, but if they are operating according to their proper natures they should not express themselves feverishly. Serenity, though found in its perfection among the saints, is not the prerogative of any one category: the same law touches the artist, the man of affairs, the educationist and the mystic. The practical aim in the case of each is rest in the appropriate activity, and the accompanying obstacles are consequently strain, false emphasis, and the over-elaborate. Where the saint preaches tranquillity of life, the artist preaches tranquillity of design. Where the artist stresses directness in treatment and effect, the saint does the same in his dealings with mankind. You may call this integrity, sincerity, or simplicity; it is all one.

To sum up. Beauty, even created beauty, must always be somewhat withdrawn, always a little bit aloof and on a throne. It is not inhuman or cold, but it has to guard itself against the vulgarity of man. It is there, on its own terms and in its own right, for any man who cares to look. There must be reverence in man's gaze, and no man may hoard his vision for himself. There is surely nothing to surprise us in these conditions when we consider from whom true beauty comes. Its terms and its rights are God's, and God is simply demanding homage to Himself — from the best that is in man.

# SIMPLICITY IN PRAYER

E HAVE SEEN THAT rightly ordered energy, whatever the form it takes, can be relied upon to run smooth and even. We have seen also that rightly ordered effect, whatever the force behind it, is inclined to spurn the frills and decorations. If this is true in regard to outward things, how much more in regard to inward? If a certain mental chastity is required of the man who paints, how much more of the man who prays? Not only does the man of prayer have to see, with the artist, beyond the production of nature and the skill of man, but he must so pay homage to what he sees that there are no side-issues, extravagances, pious flourishes, literary elaborations, unnecessary intellectual complications to distract from the main direction of his effort. His prayer, in short, must be simple.

To arrive at that simplicity, which according to all the authorities (and particularly those of the Benedictine tradition, beginning with St. Benedict himself) is so necessary to prayer, the soul must both be itself and forget itself at the same time. This is not a joke, it is a fact. It is not a trick, it is a habit. Once the soul has grasped the fact, and at least started to try and acquire the habit, quite half the ordinary obstacles to prayer are done away with. This statement calls for further consideration.

In order to be itself the soul does not have to worry too much about self-knowledge. There is a right and a wrong kind of self-knowledge — but mostly wrong. Certainly in the matter of prayer, self-knowledge is more likely to be a hindrance than a help. Perhaps if we could know *all* about self it would be a different thing, but since we never get further than finding out little bits about ourselves and the workings of our minds, the less we allow ourselves to be caught up in this absorbing study the better for both our prayer and our general recollection. The ideal is to transcend self, not to know it. Whatever knowledge of self is necessary will come to us far more safely if we make it our object first to know God. It is in Him that we see ourselves reflected for what we are. Which is not much.

There are some who would insist that a man has to know himself in order to be himself, and that without knowledge there can be no true conformity. Against this we would hold most strongly that for purposes of prayer the reverse is nearer to the truth, and that it is only by forgetting itself that a soul can effectively *be* itself. The introspection by which souls strive to come to a knowledge of themselves is fatal to pure prayer. How can a soul who is possessed[*] with the idea of understanding its inner workings be sufficiently

---

[*] Like Matthew Arnold.

detached from its own conceptions during prayer? Will it not always be questioning its motives, examining its methods, testing its reactions, probing, regretting, wondering, and in effect circulating in narrowing circles round and round the wholly unimportant pivot of self? Prayer is not meant for this sort of thing at all. Prayer is not something tortuous and self-regarding, it is something direct and outward-looking.

"Surely you are meant to tell God about your needs, about your temptations, about even your hopes and speculations: Would not all this involve a certain amount of raking about inside?" There is a difference between exposing your needs and exhibiting them. Certainly we are right to take our difficulties to God in our prayer — the whole weight of Christian tradition teaches that we should — but it is one thing to entrust a difficulty to God, asking for the grace of its solution, and another to go over our difficulties in our own minds during prayer, hoping thereby that we shall be able to find a solution of our own.

Prayer of the heart and mind, then,[*] is intended to be a loving gaze at God and not a businesslike sorting out of self. So far as self-understanding goes, the ordinary working knowledge which most of us have already is quite enough; if we try to acquire any more of it we shall end up by gazing at self and not at God . . . and even on those occasions when we have

---

[*] We are not considering here the prayers which we say aloud or read out of a book.

managed to escape from self and are occupied with God there is the danger that we shall be thinking of Him only as an extension of ourselves. No, if simplicity is one of the requirements for prayer, and if truth and confidence are its conditions, then the best possible disposition for its exercise is that which shows the least preoccupation with self. "Can any of you, for all his anxiety, add a cubit's growth to his height? . . . do not fret . . . you have a Father in heaven who knows that you need these things . . . do not consider anxiously what you are to say or how you are to say it; words will be given you . . . do not use many phrases . . . your heavenly Father knows well what your needs are before you ask him . . . if thy whole body is in the light, with no part of it in darkness, it will all be lit up as if by a bright lamp enlightening thee."

On a July afternoon three young monks, not yet priests, were bicycling along the north Devon coast road between Porlock and Lynton. Somewhere on the cliffs above Lynmouth they got off their bicycles, sat down on the bleached grass (for it was an almost tropical summer that year), and discussed prayer.

"My ideal of prayer," said one, "would be to lie out here in the sun, day after day and away from all contact with the world, and contemplate the Being of God. Just the sky and the sea and my own soul. No exams to work for, no choir practices, no manual labour . . . nothing." The speaker paused, and the three of them looked out over the empty sparkling Atlantic as if it held a secret which they had not been able to get out of their Father Baker and their St. John of the Cross and their novice-master. "The very occasional flight of a gull," went on the same young monk (a seagull had settled on a rock some two hundred feet below them), "and the gentle lapping of waves would be a help rather than a distraction: they would take the mind on from the natural to the supernatural, from space and time to limitless eternity. What about you two?"

"To me the ideal would be," said the second member of the group, "to get myself bricked up in a sort of niche or very small tribune overlooking the Blessed Sacrament exposed. It would have to be in a monastic church because I should want to hear the Divine Office going on in the background, and it would have to be so arranged that nobody could see me and that I could see nobody else." After pausing for a moment, he added: "And when I say bricked up, I mean bricked up. No bells to answer, no vestments to put out at a moment's notice. And you?"

"I would like to be locked in a cabin trunk," began the third monk when he had had a little time to consider the matter, "with just enough air (let in through holes in the lid) to allow me to breathe. I would have to be very ill — aching in every limb with a fever of some sort and a raging temperature — but still not quite unconscious or delirious. I would need to have just enough presence of mind to accept my condition as the will of God and unite my little discomforts with the Passion.

Yes, I think that's all. Except" — and here he looked at the other two and not at the Atlantic — "except that to complete the picture I'd have to have the guilty feeling that somehow it was my fault, and that really I should be doing sacristy work or going to choir practice or sitting down to *De Trinitate* or answering bells."\*

Well, that was all very nice. It was probably the sort of conversation which had taken place dozens of times before among earnest young men, and has taken place since. The particular conclusions arrived at in the discussion were not likely to do anybody any harm. Nor are they cited here as being likely to do anybody any good. As ideals for prayer, the question of their edification or disedification does not come up; all we are concerned with here is that as ideals for prayer they were wrong. However uplifting a picture you may conceive of a person praying, you are still not much nearer to the nature of true prayer. Edifying ideas about what it may feel like to pray well are no criterion.

If the conceptions above alluded to show anything, they show three distinctly individual points of view: each man seeing prayer in terms of himself and as a reflection of himself. Compare this with the wholly objective approach of the saints. What we have been calling simplicity might equally well be taken to mean objectivity. The saints, in order to illustrate the same idea — namely response to the influence of

---

\* Then they rode on and had an enormous tea in the Doone Valley.

grace — chose inanimate objects for their comparisons;[*]
they knew that so soon as a soul thinks of prayer as
being the way in which a man might feel during it, he
forgets about God and is back once more at himself.

"Yet when you turn to our Lord," a critic might argue,
"you find Him speaking about a man who calls another
from his bed in the middle of the night, of a woman
pleading with a judge, of another woman sweeping her
cottage, of a son who asks his father for an egg. Our
Lord is talking about prayer, and the models which
He chooses are alive. How, on your theory, do you
account for that?" Simply by suggesting that these
examples were chosen by Him not to teach us about
the nature of prayer but to tell us what to do regarding
it. They represent instructions in perseverance.
When on the other hand our Lord spoke about the
life of grace, which is the life of prayer, He was just
as purposely impersonal as were the saints who were
to come after Him and interpret Him. In His lessons
about the operation of grace within the soul, about

---

[*] Witness St. Teresa with her citadel, her tablet of wax, her garden, her mansions; witness St. John of the Cross with his pane of glass, his fire, his log of wood; witness St. Francis of Sales with his innumerable little similes from nature. There are exceptions of course, but the general tendency among the saints will be found to favour the strictly material for purposes of exemplifying the strictly spiritual. It is the same in the writings of those not listed among the saints but labelled simply as mystics. We have Dame Julian with her hazel-nut, Brother Lawrence with his fruit-tree. The catalogue could be extended indefinitely.

the development of the prayer life, He put before us the seed, the mustard-tree, the leaven and the harvest. For the moment He wanted to take our attention away from people and focus it upon things.

"To get back to the story of the cliff," our critic might pursue, "what these immaturely conceived images may have lacked in simplicity, they surely made up for in sincerity. At least you must give them that. You have admitted that these people's ideas of prayer were fashioned by their ideas of themselves. Which, according to the general tenor of this book, is sincerity itself." Certainly the three of them defined their ideas about prayer by advancing ideas about themselves; but surely they had idealised ideas about themselves. Each glamourised self, and to this extent each was untrue. Sincere, by all means, in the sense of being in good faith and in giving what was a genuine opinion. They projected what they believed to be themselves. But in thinking about prayer it doesn't do to project one's imagined self. The three in question would, as we have seen, have given a far more accurate picture if they had deliberately avoided projecting themselves. They would probably agree today, in their middle-age (and in their experience of failure so far as they are concerned, and, let it be hoped, success as seen in other people), that prayer is a very different business from feeling remote from the world, concentrated on the Blessed Sacrament, or resigned to considerable discomfort. Far better take the lead of the Gospel and the saints: forget about your reactions altogether, and if you are going to make use of mental images, be sure that they are drawn from the things which have no feelings. Nothing misleads like feeling. Given a chance, it can spoil almost anything.

# SIMPLICITY IN EVERYTHING

RISING OUT OF THE IDEA that simplicity is closely connected with objectivity, the further implication suggests itself that the two together are often the reason for some people's influence with others. Concluding that three of the main qualities so far discussed—truth, fidelity, forgetfulness of self—are virtually facets of the same good, we come to examine now the effects which these things have upon the world outside ourselves. If simplicity has come to mean naturalness, integrity, the main interest away from self (whether in God or in people), it is worth noting both what form it takes and what return it brings. Allowing the above hypothesis, the propositions opened up are many. Some of these are obvious, some not so obvious. For example it means that people who are wrapped up in themselves cannot be of much help to others, and at the same time are not likely to be either happy or holy in their own lives. It means that inconsistent people can never be quite natural, and that natural people are normally both out-going and receptive. It means that selfishness makes for complication within as well as without, and that hypocrisy not only attacks truth but kills it: it

kills the good which its pretence is attempting to ape. But whatever way you look at it, the key to the whole thing is truth.

Even fidelity to a good which has no direct relation to God is in a way something sacred. Certainly it is the best disposition for the reception of grace, and certainly too it is a quality which cannot but radiate influence. Although there may be nothing else in man's character which he positively imparts, the mere fact that he is sincere is an invitation to respond. In Dostoevsky's book *The Idiot*, the central figure, Prince Myshkin, is an inept person in every way; he muddles and can do nothing for himself; he appears to have no gifts. Never tempted, on this account, to play a part or think well of himself, he remains entirely simple. This fidelity to his nature, a nature which is made up, so far as rating talent goes, of the humblest qualities, elicits confidences from everybody. Dostoevsky's thesis is that pride separates people from one another and that humility unites. In this way humility is found to do the work of charity, and charity supplies for whatever else is wrong. It is as if consistency welded the two together. Charity and humility. But this is after all what one would expect: if charity is the most necessary virtue, it must be attacked by the primary vice. Pride attacks charity just as surely as it attacks humility. If Lucifer's pride divided charity in heaven, Adam's pride brought the same conflict down to earth. The division has taken place, and it is only by grace that the parts can be brought together again. Man's nature split up, disintegrated, with the committing of original sin. It has to be reintegrated. The stitches have to be picked up all along the seam. Each virtue has to be introduced again into its proper place in the pattern. Obedience where there was disobedience, humility where there was ambition, control where there was greed. They all become one in love. Multiplicity, in short, gives place to simplicity. The thing becomes a consistent whole. Which is what we have been talking about all along.

# SOME PRACTICAL CONSEQUENCES OF THIS

*L*EAVING ASIDE HIS SPIRITUAL and moral life for a moment, we can see that a man's social, intellectual, and working life will be affected by the degree of integration to which he attains. The repercussions of this doctrine are manifold indeed. It is easy to see how the social life is affected, for if the whole system of human intercourse rests on trust and truth, the satisfaction which a man finds in people is largely measured by how far he is what he says he is. That is why, when he strives after effect, his relations with others break down: it means that for the time being truth has got lost, and that consequently there is a lack of mutual trust. It is a just retribution that when a man jumps out of his element and tries to cut a figure, he doesn't jump into the limelight but into the dark.

In a recent radio discussion between young people the question was raised as to why it was that one's attraction towards another person should so often produce either dumbness or artificial exuberance. The answer given was simply the obvious one of straightforward shyness — that the effort to show up to good advantage had a paralysing effect upon one's real self, and that one either sheltered in silence or else desperately put on an act. The subject was left at that and new points were proposed. But surely under these particular conditions shyness is not the whole story. Shyness has been discussed on an earlier page, but even if we had not already gone over that painful ground there would be no need to do so here. The reason why people are not their real selves when they are romantically attracted is not *primarily* because they are shy — they may be completely un-shy subjects — but because they are not yet sure of the other person. If they were sure, there would be no need to be either on the defensive or a little bit better than their best. Later on, when they are sure of each other, and when they have had time to be sure of their own reactions to each other, the safety-curtain (or the painted drop-scene as the case may be) is rolled up. It is not because they have got used to one another's characters — they may not have — but because they have got used to knowing where they are with one another. Truth brings out confidence, and confidence brings out truth. Consequently where there is a want of confidence there is an attempt to compensate for the corresponding want of, or supposed want of, truth by being possessive or by indulging jealousy. The tendency to cling is simply due to lack of confidence. For as long as they feel insecure, for so long as they cannot trust, these unhappy people have to be always on the spot; the other is not allowed out of their sight. Love must be constant, yes, but not adhesive. Love must rest on something more secure than having the person within reach the whole time. What we fear always is that our dream hero will run away on his feet of clay. It would be far safer for all concerned if we left out of account our heroes' feet. We only tread on them. And not even ours are of the purest gold.

Turning now from man's relationships to his labours we notice certain effects which follow the same joint principle of consistency and truth. The first thing we notice is that the work explains the worker. It either betrays him or proclaims him; it cannot come out into the open untouched by his personality. Take for instance — since more clearly than other workers he both expresses himself and reflects truth, and because it is always easier to examine the extreme of any genus — the artist. The artist, whether he is a painter, writer, actor, or musician, is a showman of two things: he reveals himself and he reveals truth. He is genuine only in so far as he does both. That he should reveal himself humbly and with reserve is a matter for his conscience and his sense of good taste, but that he should reveal himself is as much in the nature of the case as that he should reveal beauty and goodness and truth.

It can thus be seen why the individual artist tends to pursue an individual line. If he is genuine, he must; it is his. Questions of style and subject-matter are not mere accident or affectation; they represent the mode of truth-plus-self-expression which is natural to the particular man who employs them. El Greco's extended figures are not to be accounted for by saying that these great artists must be allowed their little fads about anatomy and perspective and so on; El Greco's figures came from his inside, and he would have done wrong to have painted them differently. Truth puts these things into people, and the people have to come back again and again in order to let them out. So you get Renoir returning always to his luminous flesh surfaces, Degas to his filmy ballet-dancers, Rembrandt and Brangwyn to their contrasts of lights and darks, Turner and Lorrain and Blake to their harmonies . . . and so on. There is no getting away from it: in expressing truth the artist reveals himself; in expressing himself the artist reveals truth.

It is exactly the same with the novelist and dramatist, who are artists in fiction, as it is also with the musician and actor, who are artists in sound and movement. In using his imagination the creative author is not ignoring truth but actually fulfilling it. He is using his imagination for the purpose God had in mind when He gave it to him. And because it is his imagination and nobody else's, it is right that it should continue to reflect the same ideas and themes. His particular light on truth is so clear that he sees it everywhere. Maurice Baring with his unhappy love affairs and divided loyalties, Ibsen with his recurring conflicts between ambition and the rights of the soul, Wilde with his importance of being trivial, Shaw with his love of sanctity while pretending to cynicism (with his love of everything about St. Joan except the label "saint"), Graham Greene with his tortured souls whose guilt seems to mount up in spite of themselves and whose every step makes things more difficult, Evelyn Waugh with his young men who were meant to be undergraduates all their lives and who are disillusioned (and disillusioning) before you have got halfway through the book ... all these in their various and imponderable degrees of merit, natural and supernatural, are true artists. It is not their weakness but their strength that they repeat their significant word. They would be false to it if they didn't.*

Every man, then, is in a sense a prophet—with a burden of some sort which he is to deliver to the world. Every work of his hands is at once a gospel and an index—even if it is only, as it must be with many of us, a gospel of rejection and an index of defeat.

---

* "Books are not absolutely dead things, but do contain a potency of life in them so that they are as active as that soul whose progeny they are. Nay, they do preserve, as in a vial, the purest efficacy and extraction of that living intellect that bred them." — Milton.

# CASE-BOOK QUESTION

N A DEBATE TAKING PLACE AT one of our leading convent schools two subjects were discussed at great length, and since neither of them was satisfactorily settled it might be worth while to suggest a few relevant points for consideration. Before mention is made of the precise questions at issue, it should be stated that the discussion was a purely informal one—carried on between the hours of lights-out and midnight in a senior dormitory and without the sanction or knowledge of authority.*

The first question took the following form: how much has sex to do with the fact that apparently women cannot like men without being in love with them? If the answer had to be given in a single word, and if the term "sex" had to be understood in its restricted and ignoble sense, and if one accepted the further postulate about women being always in love with the men they liked, then the reply might suitably be: "Nothing." The

---

* During the next few days, and acting independently of one another, three of those who had contributed ideas at the symposium wrote letters to me asking my views on the questions proposed. In the present essay are incorporated some of the salient considerations touched upon rather hesitatingly in my replies.

confusion arises, even more than in the ambiguous use of the word "sex," over what is meant by "in love." Once establish this, relating "in love" to love without the "in" before it, and you can leave sex out of it. Sex has only come in to complicate the business because every book, every film, every play, every art exhibition speaks in "sexaphonics"; even most contemporary music, and certainly most of the lyrics to which it is set, is sexaphonic. Forget this side of love for the moment, and follow the distinction between loving and being in love.

Now it *may* be true, though it is asking a lot of the male mind to believe, that women love all the men they like, but it can by no means be true to say that they are in love with them. Where in a man you have the more or less clear dividing line between liking and loving, in a woman you are never quite sure that she isn't mixing up the two. The mistake is for either sex to generalise about the other.[*] In a truer sense than is generally understood the sexes are *opposite* sexes, and a penetrating insight into the reactions of one's own sex may be no help whatever in estimating the mental processes of the other. Making due allowances, however, and admitting that there must be outstanding exceptions in each genus, we can surely say that women tend to love far more people than men do, and that they are far more thorough in the way they go about it. The impression therefore given (to their own kind especially,

---

[*] Which is just what is being done here.

and even in their own minds individually) is that of indiscriminate falling in love. Hence the assumption of the sixth form debaters alluded to. But this would probably not be a true statement of the case at all. As a manifestation it means no more than that women have a greater propensity towards affection than men: they seem to have a wider range and a more tender sentiment: their capacity appears to be altogether greater. This need not have anything to do with being "in love." To love is part of one's nature; it is not part of one's nature to be *in* love. There is all the difference between a temporary condition, even though it may last a long time and rank technically as a habit, and a natural quality. What we are claiming here is that women are more naturally loving than men. This must not be taken to mean that men are by comparison heartless brutes with nothing in their make-up between a cold loyalty which passes for friendship and a hot passion which passes for love. All it implies is that the corresponding emotion in the man is both roused and expressed in a different way. If it is in a potentially more selfish way, this is not altogether his fault; it is the way he is made. The discussion of similar propositions among the senior members of a boys' school might even reveal compensating advantages. Certainly it could never be said of the male that he likes only the women whom he admits to being in love with. Indeed it is with him quite often the opposite: he finds himself falling in love with the people he doesn't like. Few women will appreciate this, and since the present reflexions are for such as opened the debate in the first instance, the idea need not be developed further.

The second subject to have aroused interest was of a somewhat different, and, if not less challenging, certainly less controversial character. Though having no necessary connection with the other, it may be dealt with here as admitting of much the same explanation as the foregoing. Why, it was asked, should contemplative vocations be found more frequently among women than among men? The answer is, again, that the woman is the more affectionate creature of the two, and that in the work of fixing the heart upon God as the supreme object of desire she is better suited, constitutionally, than the man. It is also quite true to say that because the woman's normal place is in the home, it is easier for her than it is for the man, whose natural function it is to go out and work for the support of the family, to settle down placidly within the shelter of the enclosure walls. This latter reason, however, considers chiefly the outward activity of the respective natures, whereas in an estimate of the contemplative vocation it is the inward activity or expression which claims the first examination. As in the first question, so in this: the man is in no serious need of having to have excuses made for him. What, for purposes of leading the contemplative life (which is by no means the same thing as practising contemplative prayer), the man may lack in the way of natural advantages, he may easily make up for supernaturally. Indeed it is claimed that though numerically the nuns show up better than the monks, it is the men contemplatives who, when you finally get down to those who are fully cooperating with the work of grace within them, can give to God a more elevated exercise. Certainly if the intellect ranks highest among the faculties, the male mind should be potentially capable of the loftier flight. *Should* be — but what do we know about things? How much do we know about the merit and measures of any one soul's contemplation as it appears before the throne of God? How much less are we able to compare one soul's contemplation with that of another, one sex's with that of another? Let the nuns have their quantitative advantage; at least there is no attempt here to give to men religious the possible qualitative advantage in contemplation. On this latter point we just do not know.

# THE GRACE OF GOD

IN THESE PAGES WE HAVE dealt largely with the difficulty which man experiences in resolving the various complexities of his nature and in finding some sort of solution to the problems of human relationship. We have seen that a formula for all this does not and cannot, humanly speaking, exist. For a man to make a success of his life, as a Christian would understand it, he needs grace. By his own unaided effort he cannot even be sure of what is wanted of him, let alone get much further once he knows. Without grace man is helpless. Without grace man is a collection of cells, tissues, and an unsupernaturalised soul which he receives through the agency of another collection of cells, tissues and a rational but unsupernaturalised soul. He is an organism functioning reasonably. If life were merely a matter of breathing in and out for long enough, eating and sleeping, *and automatically proceeding to heaven*, there would be no problem. Life, however, bristles with problems, and if their solution is to have any bearing upon the heaven to which he is designed to attain, man must be living the life of grace. Over and above the life of nature there must be that life which brings with it such things as faith, hope, and charity. It is only by grace that man can decide to practise virtue and resist vice. It is only by grace that a man can pray, can want to love God at all. Even before he can merit, before he can make the slightest claim upon God's mercy, his movements towards the supernatural are dependent upon the inspiration of grace.

Clearly the primary grace is that which enables man to believe. Once he believes in God and His plan, man finds it comparatively easy to believe that both the disturbances and opportunities which come his way are not chance happenings but are direct dispensations of Providence, and that the effort which he makes towards fitting into that plan and giving glory to God is an effort which derives its impulse from God Himself. He will not always find it easy to credit as much as this, and some of the implications will call for a measure of heroism, but the power to accept it all — and to live up to the doctrine which it teaches — will be there.

The process, then, is this. Impelled by grace in the first place,<sup>*</sup> the soul, by responding to further graces, comes readily to believe in the Trinity, the Incarnation, the Church, the Sacraments, and so. Faith, from being an act, has become a habit. The initial actual grace has been followed by sanctifying grace. Which means that the supernatural life, the life of merit and reward, is being lived.

---

\* Impelled, notice, and not compelled. There is inclination, not necessity, in the act.

Unless we allow to the operation of grace its full importance in such things as our prayer, our charity, our works which are to be of any value, our resistance to sin, we are inclined to put down too much to our own endeavour. The Apostle tells us that we cannot so much as call upon the name of Jesus without the immediate assistance of the Holy Spirit.[*]

Where the seed of this continued help is received in Baptism, the process is easy enough to follow: the seed is taken hold of, and, again with the help which comes from God, cultivated. It is in the case of the unbaptised adult that the sowing and growth of grace can, from the point of view of the soul's responsibility for the act of faith, present difficulties. Taking our stand on the fact that human beings as such are incapable of meriting supernatural gifts, and that since the grace of faith is His gift there can be no question of arriving at it by the exercise of natural qualities alone, we see that even in the most intelligent and determined of grown men and women God acts as inspiration, guide, and reward. Like a parent with a child, God steers the pen in the hand of the man who asks for grace. Once the child has got his present from Father

---

[*] Compare I Cor. xii. 3, which is commented upon by Prat, *Theology of St. Paul*, Vol. I, pp. 127-8, who says: "To confess that Jesus is Lord is a condensed profession of faith and an epitome of the Creed for that is equivalent to confessing that He is Messiah, that He is Son of God, that He is God." It is therefore necessary to receive grace before the act of faith can be launched.

Christmas, he can so use it as to gain more presents. Whatever he does about it, the present remains a present just the same. Faith first of all, and then every other virtue, is inspired in man and maintained in him by grace. Human reason may be instrumental in the process — just as human will may determine the limits to which it should develop — but so far as the supernatural goes, there is no substitute for the direct and individual act of God.

Mention of reason and will raises the question as to how far these influences contribute towards the act of faith — indeed towards any other act of supernatural virtue. An analogy may clarify the position. A bath has two taps: the hot tap represents the will while the cold represents (appropriately) the intellect. The taps are not of themselves responsible for the water which flows into the bath. The idea of water and the idea of tap are not intrinsically connected. The water does not belong to the taps. All that the taps do is to suggest a way of getting water into the bath. The labels tell us merely about the water. If we do not turn the taps we shall not be able, short of a miracle, to have a bath. It doesn't matter whether we prefer a hot bath or a cold one; the point is that there is all the water we need at the other side of those taps. For a satisfactory bath we shall probably find ourselves (whatever the intellectuals may say on the one hand, and the forthright anti-intellectuals on the other) needing to turn both taps as far as they can be made to go.

Having faith depends on God, then, just as much as having a bath depends on water. We may advance whatever argument and evidence the intellect can produce (turning on the cold tap) and we can bring to bear the full persuasion of desire (turning on the hot), but if for some reason God were to withhold His gift from us (delaying our bath) there is nothing in the world which we could do about it.[*] No water, no bath. "But at the same time," you may say, "no taps, no bath." This too is true, since the intellect and will must consent to the operation of grace, but the main object of such investigations as these is to pick on the positive and underlying principle. We think of the source of grace and the motive of faith before we start worrying about the obstacles. We are talking about getting the water into the bath, not about preventing it from getting into the bath. If grace *is* like water — and after all our Lord Himself made use of the comparison — then it is natural for us to associate it more with rivers and springs than with a certain device connected with pipes. It is our present purpose to discover where all our good comes from and how it generates in us further good; the rest of this book deals with whether or not we let it.

---

[*] The point is to this extent academic, that were a soul to continue in such excellent dispositions and with a genuine desire to receive further light from God, it is unlikely that such light would be denied.

# PENDANT TO THE FOREGOING

"FIRST ACQUIRE INDEPENdence," said a certain Greek philosopher, "and then practise virtue." In the history of philosophy there can surely be few observations to rival this one in stupidity. Though it is not worth lingering on the inversion of right order which this remark displays, it may be as well to touch briefly upon the kind of independence which the practice of virtue promotes and what should be in the mind of the individual when he addresses himself to its acquisition.

In order to understand or define independence, we must first know what dependence is. The dependent man is he who has to rely for what he wants upon things outside himself. Now if he has not yet thought of practising virtue (as understood in terms of the supernatural life and as discussed above under the heading of grace), this man has to fall back entirely upon creatures. Lacking both God and sufficiency within himself, he is dependent upon just those elements of life which are found to be the most misleading. The independent man, then, is he who rests in no earthly satisfaction whatever. Reversing the activity of the other, this one looks to the life of faith within himself as being the only possible security. He looks, in short, to God. His practice of the supernatural virtues is both cause and effect of this security. Back again, then, at the principle of grace. It is the grace which comes through Christ that makes man free. We "learn Christ," we "put on Christ," we "walk in Christ," and behold we find ourselves enjoying the liberty of the saints. Before, we were slaves to sin, to creatures, to circumstance; now, living in Christ, we are risen above self altogether and are sharing in the independence of God. "We are conquerors," says St. Paul to the Romans, "through him who has granted us his love. Of this I am fully persuaded; neither death nor life, nor angels or principalities or powers, neither what is present nor what is to come, no force whatever, neither the height above us nor the depth beneath us, nor any other created thing, will be able to separate us from the love of God which comes to us in Christ Jesus our Lord." If this isn't independence, what is? So much for the Greek philosopher's suggestion that man must wait until he has reached this stage in his spiritual development before he need think of turning his hand to the practise of virtue.

With regard to the second point, namely the nature of the mental equipment with which a man sets out upon the conscious and deliberate life of faith, we have to take up once more the question of the intellect and the will. We are back again with our bath.

First in the consent of faith, and then in the

unfolding of the spiritual life, it is the intellect which (under God) supplies the matter and inspiration, while it is the will which takes the lead. This is not the place to determine which of the two enjoys a closer union with God when the logical climax of the spiritual life has been reached — the mystical theologians themselves are not agreed — but even though God may communicate Himself at the last more to the intellect than to the will, the point to be stressed here is that in the pursuit of the spiritual life the greater activity takes place in the will. Nor, again, is it a question as to whether this spiritual life *resides* in the intellect or will — in the sense that its opposite, the material and worldly life, is said to be lived in the senses — because obviously the seat of any mental process is the intellect; the question is simply which of the two exercises the greater power and bears the greater responsibility. The answer is that the God-directed will does more and has more to answer for than the God-illumined intellect. Where reason grasps and arranges the data, the will gets the whole thing going; all the drive is in the will. It is as if, to return to that bath, the cold water were to gush out too — as a result of turning on the hot.

"I don't know anything about these fine theoretical distinctions," a critic might object, "but I do know that in practice there are people whose spiritual lives seem to contradict this view. One meets people whose religion, though perhaps solid enough in its foundations, is entirely cold and intellectual. They see that the whole thing fits in, they accept all that the Church teaches, and there their interest stops. Surely such people's faith is one of reason and not of will. There's none of this rush of steaming water into the bath; it's more a tepid trickle. Yet they are Catholics, these people, and are presumably living the life of grace. How do they stand?" Certainly to some natures the influence of argument and evidence appears to be stronger than the influence of desire. The bare fact of God, the validity of His claims, the objective truth of His revelation, seem to keep them going. On the other hand it must be remembered that if their religion were purely one of reason and not of desire at all, if it were academic only, it would not keep them going. They would cease to practise it because there would be no will to practise it. The fact that such souls persevere is evidence of how powerfully their wills are working. The will, far from playing a less significant part in these people than in their more obviously driving and willing fellow-Catholics, may be doing as much as any apostle's. It is precisely because they have been granted so little appetite, so little enterprise and interest with regard to religion's recognised forms of expression, that their deliberate and continued service of God must be very meritorious indeed. It is, in effect, the life of faith. This is not the life of pure reason, it is the life of pure faith. For such a life there has to be much willing—more willing than reasoning.

To conclude. The balance is determined not by the

weight of felt impetus but by the weight of actual motive. Felt impetus might be due to emotion and nothing more. Though impressive to look at in the scales, emotions have not the same pressure as motives. Certainly they should not be allowed to have. Motive on the other hand, carried through to execution on the initiative and labour of the will, is all the better for its being logical and cold. If a man goes on being religious for no other reasons than those of wanting to fulfil the obligations imposed upon him by the Church, of wanting to satisfy a well-informed conscience, of wanting to comply with the requirements of revealed truth, or simply of wanting to be faithful, it means that, perhaps without knowing it and certainly without any very great sense of satisfaction, he is turning on the hot tap for all he is worth. It isn't his fault if the water runs cold.

# EXAGGERATION

SENSITIVE AND TOO INTROSPECtive people are apt, without in the least falsifying their experience or even doing anything to stir the waves of their emotion, to make heavy weather. Ordinary sorrows—if sorrows can ever be ordinary—upset them more than they should, and the cross, instead of being a grace as it is designed to be, becomes a dead weight upon their spiritual progress. These souls, because the skin of their spirit is too delicate, become so bruised by the wear and tear of life that there seems to be no room for anything else. The claims of other people, the possibility that there should be such a thing in the world as joy, the acknowledgment of God in created beauty, are alike passed by because the eye of the spirit is riveted upon self and its miseries. This means that a whole section of the spiritual life—and it is a necessary section in that it represents one of the four aspects of worship—is virtually missed out; gratitude, when one feels that there is nothing to be grateful for, becomes a somewhat academic exercise. Gratitude, like generosity, is more than an obligation to be fulfilled; it is one of the forms taken in the expression of love.

From being, in the good sense of the term, interior souls, people can allow themselves to become introverts.

Often it is the fault of their spiritual director. Not that they are encouraged in the confessional to be self-pitying, suspicious, self-conscious and sterile, but that they are not given anything to take the place of self. People who may have melancholy in the blood can, by having their prayer turned upwards instead of inwards and their interest trained upon the many instead of upon the one, be prevented from becoming misanthropes and spiritual hypochondriacs. Directors, whether from motives of gentleness or indifference, are sometimes slow to impart such training. Incidentally they would save themselves a lot of trouble in the long run if they were not.

"Beware, Sammy," the elder Mr. Weller advised his son, "of whiners." The Gospels and the Epistles bid us live as saints, not as martyrs. There is no make-up more disfiguring to the soul than the mask of injured acceptance. The trouble is that frequently it is not a mask at all but a genuine expression. No blame, necessarily, to people for being unhappy, or even for being weighed down by objectively trivial cares; the blame is for showing it. Whether they show it or whether they don't, unhappy people should realise that there is no virtue in unhappiness as such. "Be you perfect" is the Gospel injunction; not "be you perfectly wretched."

Towards God this excess is shown by an attitude which, if it never quite reaches declared resentment, suggests that the soul feels itself to have been put upon; it is shown towards people by the tendency to misinterpret. Where the spiritual life and its attendant sufferings are felt to be an unwarranted imposition, a taking advantage on God's part of one's original generosity, a development which has turned out to be more than one had bargained for, there can be no spontaneity, no true liberty of spirit, no understanding of what is meant by the gift of piety. It is a complete inversion: it means that all the emphasis is being laid upon what the soul is asked to endure, what the soul is doing in the way of service, what the soul had expected the programme to be, what the soul believes would be the best thing to do next, and so on. So far as the soul is concerned it does not matter in the least what its feelings are on these subjects: the one consideration should be what God feels about it. If God is applying the spiritual life as a bewildering and painful pressure to the soul, and not as a soothing poultice, He is presumably accompanying His action with all the graces necessary. Where these self-regarding people make the mistake is in the assumption that they have nothing but their own strength to draw upon and that God is pledged to keep them abreast of His plans from start to finish.

Turning to the form which exaggerated sensitiveness takes in man's dealings with his fellow men, we see that it is summed up in the tendency to put harsh, and often self-reflecting, constructions upon the attitudes and actions of even the best of friends. People who are continually feeling that they are being hardly used by God will naturally drop into the same habit of mind when it is a question of the treatment which they are receiving at the hands of others. Most of us are the same towards people as we are towards God, but because the occasions of misinterpretation (and the grounds for it) are so much more frequent with regard to people than they are with regard to God there is greater scope for our complaints about being victimised, about having our affections rejected, about suffering our most intimate feelings to be exposed and trampled upon by those whom we had counted as our friends. Also there is more publicity attached. Nobody listens (willingly) to souls who wonder plaintively why God should be treating them so. People do listen to the story of a third party's ingratitude. They listen, not necessarily because they are moved to sympathy for the narrator, but because they like to hear of other people's failure. There is this fatal flaw in the make-up of man that uncharity has an appeal, and men will stop in their stride to hear an account of it. The tale of loyalty betrayed seldom fails to find an audience, and the self-commiserating soul takes advantage of the fact. The advantage gained is slight, because, as we have suggested, the pity is not likely to be profound. The record of patient suffering, particularly if it is unmerited and caused by someone's heartlessness or neglect, is more moving to listen to than almost anything else. But not if it is told by the sufferer himself.

# THE MUFFLED CONSCIENCE

LEFT TO THEMSELVES FOR twenty minutes in a strange place with nothing to do, people's first thought is how to make themselves comfortable. The reason why consciences fail to operate is because their owners physically and mentally pamper themselves. Very few souls are found to lapse from the faith on account of their having seen an aspect of truth which appears more convincing than what is taught by the Church; people cease to practise their religion because they submit to the a-moral, a-Christian, a-disciplined atmosphere of the world and to their own crass laziness. Conscience cannot stand up indefinitely to this willingness to submit. Spiritually we are in a strange place while living in this life, and if we look round for a principle or a philosophy or a creed which will do no more than make us feel comfortable we shall not be entirely satisfied by the facilities offered us by the Church. Making people comfortable is not after all what the Church is for.

Where religion is looked upon, not as a primary duty laid upon all mankind, but as an act or habit of supererogation, there is bound to be a whole crop of distortions, inversions and misconceptions. Inevitably people will think that by being good they are conferring a favour upon God, that the service of religion is for those who have a taste for it, that prayer exists for purposes of bringing consolation, and that whenever there is any conflict between Divine Law and human happiness it can be assumed that God is only too pleased to waive His claims. The assumption is, in other words, that man does not exist for the glory of God, but that God exists for the convenience of man. *Of course*, on such an hypothesis, God must be ready to suit His laws to man's ideas of happiness. If human felicity is all that God wants for man, then clearly there is no point in keeping the commandments which do not promote it. "God's will is my happiness, and *vice versa*," says the soul, and cheerfully marries wife after wife. *Of course*, on such an hypothesis, God must regard it as a particular favour done to Himself whenever man shows any interest in religion or any signs of obeying Him. "I'll give God a nice surprise," says the soul in effect, "and go to church on Sunday." The implication is that God is always marvelling at the extraordinary thoughtfulness of man. "I should consider Myself fortunate," God is made to say, "that My creatures are as charming to Me as they are." In so many words it seems ridiculous; it is the kind of idea which a good number of people act upon nevertheless.

It is because the faithful have wrapped up their minds in cotton-wool that they have to be enticed, pushed, milk-canned towards good: goodness no longer appeals on its own merits. The conscience is muffled.

The conscience thuds occasionally, but it doesn't jab and scream any more. The faithful should not have to be wheedled into saying their prayers, invited to Mass and the sacraments, coaxed into having their children educated in Catholic schools, almost lured into promises about the avoidance of birth-control. Conscience should be doing all this, insisting with a voice which is not questioned for a moment. If conscience fails to raise more than a tentative whisper, more than recommendation, more than an experimental suggestion, it means that the world has won and that the soul is taking its standards and instructions from the unbelieving majority. "The Church may be the true Church all right," says the soul, "and I wouldn't seriously deny its right to tell us what to do. But somehow I can't feel that any of these things are so vitally important. After all the people one mixes with don't have to etc...." And it gets back to other people's consciences, not one's own. Particularly it gets back to the consciences of people who have not been baptised in the Faith nor pledged to the code of conduct to which we as Catholics have been pledged. In comparing consciences, it is hardly ever our practice to hold them up to the light of those which evidently work better than our own; we prefer to compare them with those which are still more muffled by worldliness and unbelief.

"Oh no, you are being too hard on me," comes the answer to this outburst; "I am not as bad as that. I have no illusions about myself. I know that I should be a much better Catholic, but on the other hand provided I *am* a more or less practising Catholic, and provided I don't do any particular harm to other people, I really can't feel that I am to blame if I don't happen to have a very conscientious temperament. We can't all be conscientious *all* the time, and in any case I am quite sure God understands." The number of half-heresies lurking in such a statement is about in equal proportions to the number of half-truths. Suffice to note here that in the first place one cannot be a Catholic all on one's own, and that merely not doing any active harm to others is no sort of contribution towards one's membership in the mystical body of Christ; in the second place a soul is to blame if the conscience is not operating — just as much as a baptised soul is to blame if the habit of faith is not operating; and in the third place, though it is true to say that God understands our weaknesses and makes allowances for them, it would be absurd to say that there were certain weaknesses which, because they were found in certain people who more or less meant well when it happened to suit them and who were so indifferent to the claims of His love that they didn't feel any real sense of guilt when they transgressed His signified wishes, God would not count as weaknesses at all. It is pathetic how even those who by grace have been woven into the very texture of Catholicism can manage to sit back and begin to unstitch themselves, with the smiling assurance of good faith, from the seamless garment of Christ.

# IMPLICATIONS OF THIS

WE HAVE JUST SEEN THAT the wish for an indeterminate lightweight system of sanctification is no substitute for obedience to the code of conduct laid down by God and the Church. It is not enough to have the warmest goodwill towards man and the most generous ideas about God's power to understand human nature, if one is at the same time too indolent or too proud or too timorous to practise this goodwill, and too deliberately unseeing to notice God's other attributes. There is no excuse for not knowing what it is that we owe to man and God: both obligations are defined and promulgated. The law of charity is to be understood positively, the law of worship literally. Neighbours are to be helped by example, prayer, advice, material assistance; God is to be worshipped in His way, according to His instructions. Towards others must be shown what is now called the tow-rope philosophy, towards God the willingness to submit and accept. To this simplification there are only two things to be added by way of comment and qualification. The first is that there must be a balance between the two responsibilities, the second that there must be a right standard of assessment when coming to judge the results.

Where there is not an even balance between what is given to God and what is given to man — where in practice the two charities are pursued *as* two charities, separate and rival, instead of as one — there is bound to be waste of one or the other. If love of God and love of neighbour are not seen together, each measured by the other, each helping out the other, each expressing and reflecting the other, there will be a return to self under the cover of the gift. It is not here a question of which aspect of charity is the more important (because our Lord has left no room for doubt upon the matter), but of how to combine the exercise of each so that the combined activity of both may declare the single principle of love and not dissipate it. In proportion as the order is disturbed the principle loses its purpose. Consequently when all the weight is laid upon the one to the exclusion of the other there cannot but be love of self instead of love of charity. It is therefore the responsibility of the man of prayer to examine himself upon his outward charity. He must remember that having given everything to God, he has the more, not the less, to give to men. In the holocaust of himself which he offers to God, he must be careful that his love of humanity isn't burned away. By the same token it is the responsibility of the soul who is given over to good works to remind himself that in giving so much of his service to God's creatures he has all the greater opportunity in the direct service of divine love. In other words he must be careful not to hang himself with that tow rope.

Turning now to the other point, we need to know what to look for as a criterion of the rightly ordered life. Straight away it must be insisted that human happiness is *not* the test. If enjoyment of God's gifts on earth were the final end of man, then certainly the degree of attainment would be measured by man's happiness. But as things are, with life in God as the final end, present happiness is at best only a sign of general integration: it is not the necessary effect of moral or even saintly action; still less is it the sole justification for moral or saintly action. It is a consoling, but not invariable, by-product. And that is all.

Unhappiness, consequently, is not a sign of reprobation or of failure to meet the call of grace, or of being wrapped up in oneself. It may well come as a result of neglecting the claims of conscience, of thinking about oneself before all others, of snatching at the wrong sort of pleasures and so on, but in itself unhappiness is not particularly the sign of anything. Why are people unhappy? Surely not always because they cannot get what they want—or else everyone would be unhappy—or because they are wicked or morbid or indulgent to their melancholy. People are unhappy *because they either don't know what they want or else don't get much fun out of what they think will do instead*. Happiness and unhappiness, therefore, are relative qualities not essentially connected with the moral law and the life of grace, and not to be taken as absolute. The fact that man's nature craves for happiness, a happiness which will find its full satisfaction in God, does not alter the corresponding fact that his present felt enjoyment is not necessarily in proportion to his actual and hidden achievement.

Yet even when one has said all this, one is forced to the admission that of course it all depends upon what you mean by present happiness. If you mean, as probably most people do mean when they think of happiness, the state of mind which sails through life without a care in the world and is always able to enjoy the jollier side of whatever happens to be going on at the moment, then the above proposition holds. Happiness of this sort, we would affirm, may be a signal favour from heaven (indeed it is difficult to think of it as anything else) but it is still not the criterion of moral action. The soul still may not say: "Well, you see, I'm even as happy as *that*. What's more, I've kept it up for years. So it *shows* I was right to leave the Church." It shows nothing of the kind. All it shows is that God has not punished you in the most obvious way but has been more than ordinarily generous to you instead, and that you for your part must have a hide like a rhinoceros. If, on the other hand, by happiness is meant something quite different from the enjoyment of life, something not to do with pleasure at all, something which endures readily (though not necessarily gaily) the afflictions and disappointments and bewilderments which come along, something not so much connected with good spirits as rather with serenity and what

Mr. Cecil Beaton calls, somewhat preciously, the quiet continuum, then yes, let it be admitted, this *is* a sign of grace. It may not be an infallible sign, and a good deal of it *may* be due to natural and not supernatural dispositions, but if you are looking for tests which will prove the authenticity of moral action, this, as an indirect witness, is a far surer one to go upon than the other. Why? Because there is more evidence here of the soul's acceptance of the will of God. The whole issue, in the last analysis, hangs upon the willingness on the part of the soul to do and suffer the will of God. If perseverance in this will to receive life as God sends it, to contribute with whatever generosity one can muster, to trust that He will supply what is wanting, to keep out of mischief as far as possible, brings with it the kind of contentment which we have called, under one head or another, "happiness" — well and good. But if it doesn't, no matter. The main thing is the will of God. "Seek ye first the kingdom of heaven, and all these things shall be added."

# GIVING

THERE MUST SURELY COME A stage in most people's lives—perhaps it can be pinned down to a particular moment—when the realisation dawns upon the soul that the secret of life lies in the act, repeated and eventually habitual, of giving. Whether this perception is lived up to or not, whether it is ever formulated or even remembered very clearly, the realisation represents a chance. Thus a soul may go along for years with no plan or philosophy beyond a toe-the-line assent to the requirements of charity and religion. Then comes the grace to see what giving means. It is not a revelation in the sense of being a mystical experience; it need not have anything to do with prayer; it is simply a new light on what should be a perfectly obvious truth. The soul now knows what it has been told but has never noticed. The Gospels are all about the idea of giving, but the Gospels have never been read properly. The life of every saint is full of it—it *is* the life of every saint—but the saints have never been taken for real people. It is the explanation of most happy people's happiness, but one has always considered the other possible explanations and has never seriously thought of this one. Christ: holy people: happy people. The link is appreciated for the first time. The evidence is unmistakable.

The implications too are unmistakable. The soul is being summoned to review its whole scale of values, to alter the orientation of its life, to put its complete trust in God, and live, indifferent to the yammerings and natterings of self, for Christ and other people. It is no more and no less than the call to sanctity. Unmistakable though they may be, the implications are not compelling. No argument ever is. The will compels: the irrefutable argument doesn't. Not even grace compels — one sometimes wishes that it would — and if the combined force of grace and logic and indisputable evidence can still be resisted by the obstinacy of the human will, certainly the influence of example and invitation cannot be counted upon to break down all reserves.

Even allowing that we have recognised the need for giving — a giving which is to be incessant and all along the line of our horizon — there is the warp in fallen nature to be countered and provided for. In the matter of giving to others we can all too easily, as has been suggested in the section on marriage, give the wrong thing and in the wrong way. We may, ideally, carry our heads high and turn our faces to a cloudless heaven, but we cannot escape the fact that our feet are embedded in a rough red earth. There is a curious poem by Scott-Moncrieff, which is too good to be quoted incorrectly from memory and not good enough to be searched for in libraries, where attention is drawn to the way in which the lily, the queen of flowers, draws the material of its beauty from nothing more elegant than garbage and manure. In our mutual self-giving there is always a lurking danger that we shall forget what the rotting matter of our fallen humanity is able to produce in the way of lilies. Perhaps it is that having given so much we feel entitled to so much back. Having subscribed generously we expect an interest on our donation — which means that we want the capital as well as the interest. Thus by the end of it we have come to reverse the process and are taking with both hands. Always, then, there is this necessity of redirecting our desire, restating our purpose. Otherwise our desires will turn against us, destroying in our souls the one desire which really matters. Always it is the same conflict between the lower and the higher desire, neither able to eliminate the other and each with its determining place in the final judgement. Our desires are ourselves, and we are our desires: we can no more escape from the slide-rule of what we will than our choice can escape from us. In our relations with others, therefore, it is inevitable that our giving will take its colour from the kind of things we want, and that what we want will be determined by the quality of our giving. If to give and not to ask for a return is the ideal, it is also in practice the most rewarding thing to do.

It is the same when we give to God. Asking of us the gift of self, He rewards us with something infinitely more worth while than what we gave. Those who yield most and demand least are those who do best. Our Lord said that this would be so, and the experience of man has never contradicted it: those who have lost their lives have found them, those who have given have received a hundredfold. Yet in spite of this there are comparatively few among the millions of mankind who take advantage of the offer. Strange that we should be able to see a thing so clearly, that we should have witnessed the proof of it, that we should even feel a great longing for it, and still do nothing about it. It is not that we don't believe, and it is not that we don't think we can; it is that we are not sufficiently generous to try. We don't, in effect, give.

# GIVING IN PRAYER

*T*HE SOUL, IN AN ASCENDING scale of value, loves God in one of three ways: either with the love of resigned acceptance, or with the love of tepid preference, or with the love of extended invitation. The three ways, which are not fixed courses from whose track the soul cannot depart but which are on the contrary progressive stages which the soul is intended to mount, represent three degrees of giving: giving consent, giving priority, giving welcome. Self is given in each, but not the whole of self. Only when the surrender has both incorporated every part and been made with the cheerful intention of never going back on the act of absolute trust in God, is the gift complete and the dedication ratified. Since prayer is the field of love's expression we can now apply to the act of giving in prayer what we have considered above with regard to the act of giving in general. A paragraph may be devoted to each of the three ways of loving or—if you prefer to think of it under the other head—degrees of giving.

Acceptance of God's order is clearly the necessary condition of the whole thing. Unless, whether in prayer or out of it, there is the readiness to co-operate, the spiritual life cannot be said even to begin. The question is whether the consent is a shrug-shouldered willingness to go through with an obligation or whether it has attaching to it any warmer dispositions. You might say that acceptance of the inevitable hardly qualifies as love at all, and that it had much better be called a sense of duty. This is where prayer comes in to clarify the position: we see at once when we examine the same dispositions in prayer that acceptance of God's will very much qualifies as an act of love. Praying out of a sheer sense of duty *is* love. Resigned consent to prolonged aridity may not be as heroic as the glad yielding to whatever darkness God shall choose to send, but heroic it is nevertheless. It has in it the elements of love. It is unselfish and it is constant: with the further practice of prayer the unselfishness will develop, and the disposition will merge imperceptibly into the next grade, but even in its present state it is no mean expression of devotion. The solution which love brings to the problem of prayer, no less than to the problem of life, is not always an agreeable one — there is certainly no guarantee that it should be — so that to accept what appear at the outset to be hard terms is surely to be counted for loving service. If prayer is the appropriate expression of a soul's love for God, then resignation to the sense of one's insufficiency as well as to whatever kind of prayer God sends is, whatever may be said about making a virtue of necessity, a good enough beginning.

The next step in generosity is to be seen in the choice of God's order before one's own. Not content to wait passively for the next development, hoping against hope that it will not turn out to be as unpleasant as it probably will be, the soul repudiates its own preferences and elects absolutely for God's will. It is no longer submission, but deliberate option. "Not that I am in the least fervent about it," says the soul to God in prayer; "in fact my laziness makes me wish still that the spiritual life had never been invented. All I know is that where before I went on because I couldn't see how I could get out of it, now I go on because I choose to. I want what You want me to have — even if I can't help hoping at the same time that what You want will turn out to be the same as what I want." Whether you think this satisfies the requirements of abandonment or not, whether or not the detachment is sufficiently generous, certainly the act is one of love; it is the essential act of giving.

Finally the development takes the form of going out with all flags flying to meet the will of God. There are no reservations here, no clauses in small print (to change the metaphor from the ocean to the solicitor's office), no long-sighted and surreptitious views of possible self-interest. The motive is the love of God, the prospect is the love of God, the sustaining principle is the love of God . . . and the reward, which is also known to be the love of God, can be left in the hands of Him who grants it. This is surely the perfection of giving. Not that the soul no longer asks for things from God — there is always an element of petition in prayer, right up to the end — or that the manifestations of God's will, outside prayer as well as in, are not still felt at times to be exceedingly disagreeable. Inevitably the soul must, if it is to be true to its nature, continue to yearn for gratification of some sort, and all this will find reflexion in its prayer, but whereas before the desires were in a varying degree independent they are now subordinated and united to the paramount desire for God's will. Just as inevitably the soul must, so long as it remains a sensitive organism, go on minding the adverse things that happen to it. Indeed, in a sense it seems to mind more, it seems to become more vulnerable instead of less, it grieves with a deeper sense of desolation than before. All this, again, will have its repercussions in the life of prayer. But in this conscious sadness, expressed very clearly to God, there is now a difference: the element of self has been—just as the element of self in the case of the desires has been—sublimated to serve the will of God. The soul, more sensitive than ever, may find itself minding exceedingly the setbacks of life, may be almost reduced by them, may cry out to God as Christ cried out in Gethsemani to His Father, but none of this will be in the same spirit of melancholy. The soul may grieve, but not at all with a sense of grievance. What has happened in this third development of love or giving is that the soul has come to be efferent—bearing out—instead of remaining merely afferent as it was before. It carries its whole being forward towards God and embraces the disposition of

Providence. The forms which this disposition will take may be known or unknown, it doesn't matter which; the commitment covers the unpredictable. Nothing is felt to be altogether insupportable if God is known to be taking the strain; in the same way nothing is felt to be altogether imponderable if God is known to be holding the scales.

To conclude. The surrender of self, going further than submission and acknowledgment, which have particular regard to the actual and the immediately foreseen, means the dedication of the whole man not only to the actual but also to the unseen range of possibility as it exists in the mind of God. It means being prepared in practice to go on surrendering without the assurance that the surrender has either been accepted or is being of any use. The presents which cost us most to give are often those which leave us without our being sure that they will be valued and not despised. To feel that in our surrender we have at once despoiled ourselves, given no great satisfaction to God, been possibly deluded by self-interest from the start, and so in effect given nothing at all, is surely part of the surrender. Perhaps it is the necessary consequence of it; perhaps it *is it*. Certainly what better proof that it has taken place than the sense of having nothing now to depend upon than stark unverifiable trust? Would not an assurance rob the whole thing of its significance? Would not an assurance — we being what we are, and only too ready to lean back if there is the slightest sign that the work has somehow been completed without our noticing it—put a stop to its continuance? For if in this matter of self-surrender there is one constituent which ranks as high as that of totality, it is that of persistence. The man with his plough may not look back, the man with his pearl may not put on the market again what he has taken so much trouble to buy, the man who has dug up his treasure may not bury it again; the candle must keep burning, the seed must go on growing, the leaven must rise in the dough, the vine must spread; everywhere the force must be kept up. Generosity does not cease with the gift, love is not over with the declaration. Whether, in accordance with our threefold division, the giving is one of resigned sacrifice, of chosen sacrifice, or of longed-for opportunity to sacrifice, the soul which is set to the act is that of keeping up with it. It doesn't matter a great deal how it begins, *c'est le dernier pas qui compte.*

# THEME TUNE

IT IS A MISTAKE TO BORROW too much from the past and the future in order to buy what is thought to be happiness for the present. The present has to be paid for in the actual currency of the moment. Past and future are bank books only: they have no purchasing power whatever. We are not meant to live on stamped counterfoils and statements of balance in hand.

"But surely if I find the present disagreeable," a soul will say, "the only sensible thing to do is to remember the pleasure of the past and to try and construct from it some sort of image of the future. There doesn't seem to be any other way of building up the necessary confidence. When one has lost confidence in the here and now, one is presumably meant to find it somewhere else." Granted that there has to be confidence if life is not to be slowed down to passivity, the point disputed here is the source of such confidence. A spurious confidence is not worth having: one is left finally with a keener sense of emptiness and insufficiency than if one had never had any confidence at all. It becomes a question, therefore, not of creating the illusion of confidence, which may be considerable, but of establishing its reality, which may be insignificant by comparison. We would claim that the present, however disagreeable, must always provide this if one goes about it properly.

The moment one begins to fashion for oneself unreal worlds out of unreal—in the sense of un*actual*—material, one begins to lose the reality of the immediate, the appropriate, the true. And this, we have seen, is one of the cardinal mistakes which man can make. In practice what happens when we draw upon the future or the past? To look forward either raises hopes which, if not false, are necessarily insubstantial, or else on the other hand occasions dreads which equally have no absolute foundation. To look back is no better: the mind is first of all filled with pictures which are seen out of focus and away from their setting, and then, when the pictorial memory has spent itself, is forced to make comparisons which as a rule reflect badly upon the present. So what is the good? Why run the risk of missing the present opportunity?

"But is there always this present opportunity?" may come the question. "Are there not whole periods in our lives when we know ourselves to be so much waste material, when even if there were any sense of purpose or direction we lack the zest to carry the thing through; when the prevailing mood is one of bitterness and listlessness and regret? Times such as these are surely not actualities to be lingered in?" To answer this we need to get down to fundamentals. Given God, the soul, and the relationship between (and these are the absolute fundamentals) their *venue* in this life is bound to be that section of time which we call the present. There is only one possible meeting-place, or rather only one possible meeting *moment*, for the union of the will of God with the will of man. For so long as we remain creatures whose lives are lived out in terms of time, when else can we meet God save in the existing now? We do not belong to any other moment; no other moment belongs to us. Consequently whatever our present dispositions, whatever our misgivings or regrets or longings with regard to the past, whatever our fears or wishes or indifferences regarding the future, it is the here and now which is our particular concern, and this infallibly carries with it the opportunity of uniting our will with the will of God. *Anima mea in manibus meis semper* — to be applied to the circumstances of the moment.

If the past teaches us anything at all it is that away from God's will there can be no real peace. If our experience shows us no more than where not to place our confidence, it will have justified itself as an attribute of the past. The lesson of life should have taught us to rely neither upon our happiness, our friends, ourselves, nor the future. Reliance has to be upon God or it will disappoint us. Is this a depressing view to take? It is the view one is forced to. Nor is it so depressing when you consider that the whole burden of our argument is to the effect that the soul is invited to reflect not upon wasted opportunity but upon opportunity. Look back, we say, and you lay yourself open at once to discouragement: look forward and you wonder how you can ever persevere. The only solution is to look fixedly at the present where you have the immediate support of God's will. "What other refuge can there be," cries the psalmist, "except our God?" The need for a refuge is neither a dead one nor one unborn; it is a living need.

The habit of thinking and working in the present is like the habit of thinking and working objectively: it comes with the practice of prayer. Souls who are close to God are no longer worried by the past and the future. Where the rest of us are distracted by failures seen in retrospect, and so, by dreading lest the past should repeat itself in the future, come to waste the chances which are offered us, the saints — more detached, more objective, more confident in God's mercy and God's providence — are apprehensive about nothing save the instant necessity of conforming to the whole of God's signified will.

So whether because God eventually dries up all the streams except those that lead to Him, or because we have become immunised by our disappointments, or simply because the spiritual life produces this effect, the result is, mercifully, detachment. Never entirely free, we come less and less to rely on human consolations and affections. What neither age, nor effort, nor physical isolation can do towards our independence, Providence does for us. We know at last that nothing matters except God — and perseverance.

## ABOUT THE CENACLE PRESS
## AT SILVERSTREAM PRIORY

An apostolate of the Benedictine monastery of Silverstream Priory in Ireland, the mission of The Cenacle Press can be summed up in four words: *Quis ostendit nobis bona*—who will show us good things (Psalm 4:6)? In an age of confusion, ugliness, and sin, our aim is to show something of the Highest Good to every reader who picks up our books. More specifically, we believe that the treasury of the centuries-old Benedictine tradition and the beauty of holiness which has characterised so many of its followers through the ages has something beneficial, worthwhile, and encouraging in it for every believer.

cenaclepress.com

ALSO AVAILABLE:

Dom Hubert Van Zeller OSB
*Letters to A Soul*

Robert Hugh Benson
*The King's Achievement*

Robert Hugh Benson
*By What Authority*

Robert Hugh Benson
*The Friendship of Christ*

Blessed Columba Marmion OSB
*Christ the Ideal of the Monk*

Blessed Columba Marmion OSB
*Christ in His Mysteries*

Blessed Columba Marmion OSB
*Words of Life On the Margin of the Missal*

Visit cenaclepress.com
for our full catalogue.

www.ingramcontent.com/pod-product-compliance
Lightning Source LLC
Chambersburg PA
CBHW030258100526
44590CB00012B/436